a fresh look at **F E A R**

| DISCIPLESHIP
| ESSENTIALS

A Beautiful Way
An Invitation to a Jesus-Centered Life
by Dan Baumann

The Leadership Paradox
A Challenge to Servant Leadership
in a Power-Hungry World
by Denny Gunderson

Learning to Love People You Don't Like
by Floyd McClung

The Chicken Farm and Other Sacred Places
The Joy of Serving God in the Ordinary
by Ken Barnes

a

fresh

look

at

FEAR

encountering Jesus in our weakness

Dan Baumann

YWAM PUBLISHING
Seattle, Washington

YWAM Publishing is the publishing ministry of Youth With A Mission (YWAM), an international missionary organization of Christians from many denominations dedicated to presenting Jesus Christ to this generation. To this end, YWAM has focused its efforts in three main areas: (1) training and equipping believers for their part in fulfilling the Great Commission (Matthew 28:19), (2) personal evangelism, and (3) mercy ministry (medical and relief work).

For a free catalog of books and materials, call (425) 771-1153 or (800) 922-2143. Visit us online at www.ywampublishing.com.

Library of Congress Cataloging-in-Publication Data
Baumann, Dan, 1963–
  A fresh look at fear : encountering Jesus in our weakness / Dan Baumann.
    pages cm
  Includes bibliographical references and index.
  ISBN 978-1-57658-792-8 (alk. paper)
  1. Fear—Religious aspects—Christianity. I. Title.
  BV4908.5.B38 2014
  248.8'6—dc23   2014032175

First printing 2015

Printed in the United States of America

contents

introduction

You are special. We are special. As created beings, according to the Bible, we are the primary focal point of God's good intent. From the opening pages of the Bible, where we read the story of creation, to the end, where we see the culmination of God's purposes, we hear God's heart for us. He loves us so much, and He desperately wants us to experience the fullness of life. Nothing can put fear into perspective more than God's love! This is the simple focus of the book in your hands—encountering Jesus in the midst of fear.

Although fear is a reality in life, there is hope in God in the face of fear. Each person's journey with fear is different. Sometimes, in His mercy, God comes quickly, delivers us from fears, and changes our perspective in a moment. More often, however, God leads us through a learning process so that we can better trust Him and let go of our fears. God always gives us the hope of overcoming our greatest obstacles. That hope is found in Him alone, not in a formula, medication, or any other temporary coping mechanism, though these things can provide necessary and practical help.

My hope for you is that you would encounter the beauty of Jesus and, in doing so, discover His love to be a more compelling reality than the fear you face.

chapter one

The Reality of Fear

*F*ear is real. We all battle with it in some form or another. The good news is, God is bigger than our fears.

As I travel and speak, I encounter thousands of people who tell me that fear is one of their biggest struggles. Understanding the beauty of God, His greatness, and His goodness does not do away with our humanity; it does not completely remove fear from our hearts. Even so, our experience of God and His love has the ability to put our fears into perspective.

So in various settings, I often find myself sharing my own experiences of fear, and what I learned through them. My imprisonment in Iran marks the greatest struggle I have ever had with fear. After joining Youth With A Mission (YWAM) in 1988, I lived and traveled in Central Asia, spending several years in Afghanistan and Turkmenistan. In 1997, my friend Glenn Murray and I traveled from Turkmenistan into Iran to explore future service opportunities there. On our return journey, immigration officials detained us and, without explanation, confiscated our passports. It was then that fear gripped my heart.

Days later, we walked into the security building in Tehran to reclaim our passports. Immediately, we were separated and interrogated by officials. I remember being led up a flight of stairs into a small, dark room. When I heard the door slam behind me, fear like I had never experienced before took hold of my heart.

My interrogators began shouting at me and threatening me. "Why are you here, Mr. Baumann? You will answer us truthfully!"

I had become a slave to fear.

Every truthful answer I gave provoked more angry intimidation. The men began to kick and slap me. The abuse continued this way for three hours, until I was left alone in shock, shaking uncontrollably from head to toe. My whole body was shuddering. I could not stop my teeth from chattering. My bladder felt like it was always full. Fear had taken over.

At the time, it did not occur to me that I should be trusting in God. After a few hours, the interrogators led Glenn and me blindfolded downstairs and pushed us into the backseat of a waiting car. During the drive, we were forced to keep our heads down. My body had not ceased its trembling, and my heart was overwhelmed by fear. Every time I tried to speak to Glenn, someone shouted at us to keep silent. When the car finally stopped, we were led into another building where our blindfolds were removed.

The men who had terrorized us at the other building were still with us, and now they proceeded to take away everything we had—clothing, bags, watches, and glasses—leaving us standing in only our underwear. Finally, we were given prison clothes and, after putting them on, were led down a staircase and into separate prison cells. My interrogators shoved me into a small room, and as I stood in shock and horror, they slammed the metal door behind me. I heard it being locked from the outside.

Whatever our fears may be, when
they take over our hearts, we feel
trapped, desperate, and alone.

Alone in my cell, the reality of my situation began to sink in. Tears filled my eyes, and I prayed, "God, where are you?" I began pacing back and forth and banging on the walls. I had never felt fear so intensely in my life. I told myself over and over again, "I can't handle this! I can't handle this!" Throughout the night, I went to the bathroom every fifteen minutes, though I had not had anything to drink. I was given a plate of food, but I could not eat. I could not stop shivering, moving, or crying. The only things I felt were fear and abandonment by God. Minutes felt like hours. That first night felt as if it lasted a whole month. For three days I did not sleep, even for a minute. Every time I would lie down to rest, I was overcome with fear and was unable to relax my mind and body. I had become a slave to fear. Those first days in prison, I knew no other reality.

My imprisonment is a constant reminder to me of my weakness and frailty. That I survived and was released does not minimize how desperate and afraid I felt in the midst of it. Those days were some of the lowest and darkest in my life.

The fear was real, and it does not take much for me to remember how greatly it affected me.

I know I am not alone. I know that others have experienced fears as I did in that prison. For you, the setting may have been completely different. You may have faced another kind of torture or been threatened in other ways. Each one of us knows what it is like to feel weak and afraid. Your fears may be private, locked away in your heart of hearts. Or they may be something you have shared openly with friends, family, or counselors. Whatever our fears may be, when they take over our hearts, we feel trapped, desperate, and alone.

Faith reminds us that there is always hope,
even if fear is telling us that there isn't.

Fear is a universal part of our broken humanity. The Bible reflects this reality, portraying hundreds who are said to have known fear or to have been afraid. Adam and Eve felt fear in the Garden of Eden after they sinned (Gen. 3:8–10). Abraham felt fear when he lied to both Pharaoh and Abimelech about his wife, Sarah (Gen. 12:10–13; 20:2). Job was afraid when he lost all but his life (Job 3:25). David's psalms are filled with confessions of fear as he ran from Saul and hid in caves. When Jonah was tossed overboard and swallowed by a great fish, he was afraid, and when Peter was confronted on the night of Jesus's arrest, he too was afraid. Paul admits fear in the midst of his work as an apostle of Christ: "When I was with you, I was weak. I was afraid and I shook" (1 Cor. 2:3 NLV). These testimonies bring us comfort, reminding us that even those who are strong in faith struggle with fear. Faith in God is what pushes us to embrace our weakness and to believe that

God is present with us in the midst of our darkest fears. Faith allows us to see beyond our situations and find God, despite ourselves. Faith reminds us that there is always hope, even if fear is telling us that there isn't.

Alone with my fears, I began to contemplate how I should kill myself.

Two weeks into my imprisonment, my faith in God was at an all-time low, and I was listening only to the voice of fear. It was the darkest day of my life. I awoke that morning with a level of despair I had never known. I felt I had no reason to live. I had had fleeting thoughts of suicide during the first few days of my imprisonment, but now it felt like suicide was my only option, the only way out. Alone with my fears, I began to contemplate how I should kill myself. The sink in my cell was connected to the wall by a bracket. I saw how my towel could be tied onto one side. If I filled the sink with water and plugged the drain with my shirt, I could fully immerse my head. I could then reach around to pull the towel over my head and tie it to the bracket on the other side, holding my head firmly in the sink. I figured if I did it right, the towel would prevent me from jerking my head up out of the water even when I started to gag from lack of oxygen. Within a few minutes, I would be dead.

I wrestled for about an hour, trying to talk myself out of it. Eventually, fear won. I waited for the hourly guard inspection to pass. Then I crept to the sink and filled it with water. I tied one end of the towel to the left bracket. I stuck my head under the water, pulled the loose end of the towel over my head, and looped it through the right bracket. I pressed my forehead down to the bottom of the sink until my face was submerged. Then I hesitated. I was sure if I tied the towel in a simple knot to the bracket, my plan would work and I would be free from the misery of my fear.

Suddenly, I jerked my head out and fell to the floor, gagging and coughing. I couldn't do it. More depressed than ever, I told myself, "Come on, Dan, do it! You will be in eternal bliss. Come on, do it!" Spurred by this, I mustered the energy to try a second time. Again, I was too scared to tie the towel tightly, and as I reached the point of gagging, I jolted my head out of the water to gasp for breath. I tried a third time, then a fourth. On my final attempt, I was able to tie the towel in one simple knot. As I began to struggle, I became frantic. I desperately untied the knot and jerked my head out of the water for the last time. It was then that something within me broke. I fell to the ground in shame and began to weep uncontrollably. I could hardly believe what I had done. I was completely exhausted and broken.

In my darkest moment, in my deepest despair, Jesus had come to me.

As I lay there, with my hands covering my face, something changed in the room. Suddenly, there was more light than normal. I turned and saw a vision. Jesus was standing before me, His face shining in all its glory. It was a glorious light. He was more beautiful than words could ever describe. As I looked, I was overwhelmed by the love in His smile. He stretched out His hands toward me and reached underneath me, saying, "I will carry you through this time." In a moment, the vision ended. I was alone again, but somehow not alone. I could not describe what was happening in my heart and mind. I was overcome, this time not by fear but by love.

In my darkest moment, in my deepest despair, Jesus had come to me. In the midst of my loneliness and fear, He came to me in love, not to condemn me, but simply to accept me and to promise to care for me. It did not matter to Him how faithless or hopeless I was. I had been ready to take my life— but He was not ready to let me go. I had not taken any steps toward Him, but He reached out His hand and rescued me. As I sat and meditated on what had just happened, I became increasingly aware of God's mercy in my life. Any thought of suicide was now gone from my mind. I rested in my cell, and my heart was at peace. From that day on until today, I have never had those thoughts again. That day in my cell, Jesus rescued me from myself.

Fear is real, but God is bigger, and His love is stronger. My story is a testament to that. There is nothing in this world more beautiful or wonderful than God Himself, who invites us into relationship with Him through Jesus Christ. There is no greater hope for our broken humanity than that.

I share this story for one reason—to glorify God by affirming that His beauty and love are stronger than the reality of fear. I do not hesitate to share my weaknesses, because I believe that in weakness there is great strength. The Bible clearly states this: God says to Paul, "My power works best in weakness" (2 Cor. 12:9 NLT). In the Bible, human weakness is not only assumed; it is also embraced. The heroes of Scripture are often described as weak, fragile, and afraid. Nevertheless, throughout the Scriptures we see that God does not turn from them—He runs to them. God embraces them and gives them a hope that eclipses their fears. He continues to do the same for us today.

Jesus, thank You that Your power is greater than anything going on in my life. I am often weak, fragile, and afraid. Help me to acknowledge my weakness before You. I do not want to pretend to be stronger than I am. When I am weak, then I am strong. I believe that You have chosen me to bring glory to Your name and that Your beauty and love are stronger than my fears. Be glorified in me today. Amen.

chapter two

A Fresh Look at Fear

Only God Himself, through His beauty and His love, is able to transform our experience of fear into an invitation to deeper intimacy with Him. In this way, fear can push us to God.

Our culture teaches us that one of the greatest obstacles in life is fear. We are told that the best way to live life is to "face your fears." For some reason, we think that in order to live in the joy, peace, and contentment of knowing Christ, we must first be rid of our fear. It certainly feels like fear is our primary obstacle. But is the real goal in life to get over our fears?

Suppose you could live a life free from fear—then what? Would you instantly be filled with joy, peace, and contentment? Would you suddenly know the fullness of life that is in Jesus?

Let's look at life from three possible perspectives on fear:

1. You live in a partial state of hopelessness and accept that life is about managing fear. This is as good as it will get.

2. You reject all feelings of fear and never feel afraid again.

3. You live in discovery of knowing the God who loves you, and allow His love to place your fear into perspective.

Many people adopt the first perspective, not because they want to, but because they do not see any other way. They learn to manage their fears in such a way that they can still live with some degree of peace and contentment. The second option—living without fear—is, of course, what we say we want. But mere absence of fear isn't really what we want. When we say we want to be rid of the overwhelming weight of fear, what we're really saying is that we want to be overwhelmed by joy, peace, and contentment, no matter the circumstance.

Over the years, the third perspective has become the most intriguing to me. More and more, I am discovering that living this way is actually possible. "Getting over" fear is not the ultimate goal of faith. Living to discover and know God is. When I have been afraid, it has not been the departure of fear but the knowledge of God that has brought joy, peace, and contentment to my heart.*

---

* Now, 1 John 4:18 tells us that "perfect love casts out fear" (NKJV), and 2 Timothy 1:7 says, "God has not given us a spirit of fear, but of power and of love and of a sound mind" (NKJV). There are many ways in which God has led his people to deal with fear. Many times my friends and I have quoted truth in the face of fear and commanded fear to leave us. We have said, "Fear, be gone, in Jesus's name" or "I declare that this fear never affect me again." While it has not been the primary way in which I have seen my fears relieved, I firmly believe in direct miracles, in one moment of prayer and declaration, when God overcomes our fear. He can do it! I honor this approach of turning our eyes to Jesus and His truth. If running to Jesus and rebuking fear and declaring it "gone" has brought victory in your life, amen! Let Him be glorified in this way too, as He overcomes all fear in His perfect love.

On the journey, I've had to ask myself some fundamental questions: Is Jesus really that loving? Is His love really bigger than my fears? Does the knowledge of His love truly bring joy, peace, and contentment?

Over and over, I am discovering that the answer to these questions is a resounding, "Yes!" The love of God is that real, it is that profound. Exploring the truth about the love of God has become one of the primary ways I have learned to deal with fear in my life, because it has transformed my perspective and significantly broadened my understanding of God.

In the end, it is not the absence of fear but the love of God that we truly want.

In Revelation 3:20 Jesus says, "Behold, I stand at the door and knock; if anyone hears My voice and opens the door, I will come in to him and will dine with him, and he with Me" (NASB). Throughout the New Testament, Jesus extends the same invitation to follow and commune with Him—and He never mentions fear as a hindrance. In fact, fear should alert us to the knock of Jesus at the door of our heart. When we feel afraid, we should open the door, let Jesus in, and enjoy His company. In the end, it is not the absence of fear but the love of God that we truly want.

Ever since I was sixteen years old, I have known God's unconditional love for me. Even so, there have been ups and downs and times when I have been tempted to question the extent of that love. We can easily slip into a distorted way of thinking, which says God's love for us is based solely on what we do for Him and not purely on His grace. When I was released from prison in Iran, the only two things I knew for certain were my weakness and God's love. My experience in prison was the clearest example to me that God's love was not based upon anything I did. I knew how weak I had been during those nine weeks, and I knew how merciful God had been to bring me through it all.

---

*It is when we doubt God's love that
our fears grow and take root.*

Have you ever experienced God's unconditional love becoming unmistakably real? Just before I was released from prison, I had lost hope. I did not believe I would ever get out. My heart was empty; I had no faith that my situation would ever change. However, on March 16, 1997, I was set free. Just like that, I was let go. I knew in that moment, beyond a shadow of a doubt, that I had experienced the love of God in a dramatic way. It was an emphatic word from God that He loves me. He loves Dan Baumann, despite all of Dan Baumann's mistakes, weaknesses, and fears.

Although I do not wish the traumatic experience of being imprisoned on anyone, I do long for people to experience the love of God. There are innumerable ways that God communicates His love to us, but sometimes it takes radical experiences for us to be convinced of just how strongly He feels about us. I do not ever want to go back to prison, but more than that, I do not ever want to forget what I learned there. That experience helped me see a clearer picture of God. In the days, months, and years that followed, I only became more certain of God's beauty and greatness, and more overwhelmed by His love for me.

Paul, the apostle of Christ, was also overwhelmed by this love. He was amazed at its strength and at how absolutely nothing in the world can keep us from experiencing it. In his letter to the church in Rome, Paul writes, "I am convinced that nothing can ever separate us from God's love. Neither death nor life, neither angels nor demons, neither our fears for today nor our worries about tomorrow—not even the powers of hell can separate us from God's love. No power in the sky above or in the earth below—indeed, nothing in all creation will ever be able to separate us from the love of God that is revealed in Christ Jesus our Lord" (Rom. 8:38–39 NLT).

God's greatness is all around us, all the time,
but sometimes we need a revelation of it.

At times, it is easy to doubt God's love and instead believe that our circumstances, sins, or failures will distance or disqualify us from the love He has for us. It is when we doubt God's love that our fears grow and take root. Some of us are afraid that the powers of darkness are too strong and that we are too weak to resist them. However, Paul insists that God's love is stronger. Some of us are afraid that the worries and temptations of the world are too much for us. But God's love is bigger. Some of us catch ourselves believing that it all depends on us, and we fear we are not strong enough, smart enough, or spiritual enough to hold on to God's love. But it doesn't depend on us—our hope is secured in Him! Oh, Jesus, open our eyes! Help us see we are held fast in Your love!

Nothing, nothing is more powerful than God's love. Nothing is more dependable. Nothing in the world can steal or quench it. Nothing can dilute it, hide it, or make it unattainable for us. It is always right there, available and free. There is nothing that can stop Him from giving it, and nothing that can disqualify us from experiencing it! No failure, no fear, no financial crisis, no boss's decision, no bad grade or bad hair day, no injury or disease—nothing will separate us from His love.

Another aspect of God's character that has helped me understand His love for me is His greatness. God's greatness is all around us, all the time, but sometimes we need a revelation of it. A few years ago, some friends and I hiked and camped on Mount Whitney in central California. Before falling asleep that night, I remember looking up into the black sky and seeing thousands upon thousands of stars. They appeared in a greater multitude than I had ever seen. I was in awe at the greatness of God, who put each one of those stars in its place. How could He keep track of them? Where did they all come from? How could He give names to each one? The night sky was an incredible display of God's great power.

When I dwell on who God is, my fears lose their preeminence and become small.

Another time, in northern Finland, just outside the Arctic Circle, I had the chance to see the northern lights—an amazing natural display of light dancing across the horizon in the night sky. Again, I was in awe, and I felt blessed to experience this show of God's greatness. It was as if God, in all His omnipotence, stopped, leaned down, and said to me, "Hey, Dan, check this out!" It was a gift, a personal reminder of God's greatness.

God wants to use His power to intimately show us His love for us. He wants us to see what He has done and to enter into His joy and satisfaction. He invites us in, saying, "Hey, take a look at this!" He is not too busy for moments like that. He takes that kind of time with each one of us, if only we will give Him the chance. Seeing the northern lights in Finland was one of those moments for me to stand in awe of God's creative power and feel His personal love.

God is all-powerful and all-knowing, and He is in control of the universe. When I look at God's greatness, I realize that He will never lose the power to love. His love is forever. Even so, sometimes I struggle to believe He loves me. But the nature of God's character reminds me that His love for me is part of His very essence. "God is love" (1 John 4:8). In order for God to be love, He must have another being to love. This seems possible only in the context of the Triune God—a God who exists in three eternally distinct, yet inseparable, persons who love one another completely. This is the only way we can understand God as love. In his booklet Parable of the Dancing God, Dr. C. Baxter Kruger suggests that we think about this eternal relationship of love within the Trinity as a dance. Call it the great dance of God—pure affection, complete joy, unending gratitude, and seamless perfection forever. That is the Holy Trinity. That is God!

What about us? Where do we fit into this love, this dance? At the creation of the world, something remarkable happened. In the very midst of the great dance of eternal love, God said, "Let us make human beings in our image, to be like us" (Gen. 1:26 NLT). This is how we came to be. We were created out of this communion, with a capacity for relationship with God, and were invited to join in the dance and to enjoy the seamless perfection of His love. This is an invitation that God extends to all of humanity. Do you want to join in that dance?

If this kind of intense love is at the very core of God's being and existence, how might knowing this change the way we live and deal with fear? When I dwell on who God is, my fears lose their preeminence and become small. The overwhelming realities of God's love, beauty, and power put our fears into perspective. All we need to do is open our hearts to the God of all things and in humility admit that His love is bigger than we currently know, than we could ever know, and that our relationship with Him has only just scratched the surface.

Fear can be a distraction from being overwhelmed by God's affection for us, but it can also be an invitation to discover the same.

God is more amazing, more beautiful, more wonderful than we could ever imagine. We will never have enough time to experience the fathomless depths of His love. It is more constant than the air we breathe and more faithful than the rising sun. A lifetime is too short to explore the breadth of the beauty of God. There is no end to His love.

Fear can be a distraction from being overwhelmed by God's affection for us, but it can also be an invitation to discover the same. When I am afraid and feel compelled to get rid of the fear, what I really need to do is receive a greater revelation of God's love. We have been given an invitation to know and discover God our Father. Even in the midst of fear, we are fully loved! Not just by a God who loves us, but by a God who is love.

God, thank You for loving me. Help me understand Your love for me. Help me realize that my fears are an invitation to deeper intimacy with You. Help me see that Your love is bigger and stronger than I have known, and that I have only scratched its surface. I want more of You. I want to experience more of Your love and to see more of Your power. Overwhelm me now, I pray. Amen.

chapter three

Fear of Losing Control

We are not in control, nor were we ever meant to be. We were meant to trust. From the very beginning, the Bible gives us a clear picture of God's sovereignty. God is in control of the world that He created. Within that world, God appointed us to a prominent role. That role is not only to enjoy His goodness but also to be managers of His plan and purposes for the world. Our primary responsibility in life is to God Himself, to trust Him and follow His plan.

As I thought about writing a chapter on trust, my first reaction was, "Ouch! I'd rather not be confronted with that myself, so why would I push others to think about it?" But the truth is, the more I have learned to trust God and relinquish control, the more exciting and enjoyable my life has become. God always has something better for us.

We desire to feel in control because we want outcomes to be predictable and we want to know where we are headed. It is incredibly scary to feel as though things are slipping out of our control. It means there are things we do not have answers for. It also means we can't protect ourselves from pain and suffering. What is the root cause of our fear? I believe it stems from our not being convinced that God is a good, loving, and committed Father. Again, however, fear of losing control is an invitation to trust in God.

What if I could live in complete control of my life? Would this bring happiness?

So let's consider three possible perspectives on control:

1. Your life is a constant struggle to maintain control. When things seem out of control, you feel deeply unsettled and anxious. You feel there is no guarantee of peace or safety unless you have control.
2. You live in complete control. Life never feels overwhelming, and you always get the outcome you want.
3. You live relinquishing control and, as a result, discover the joy of completely trusting God.

Which of these three approaches delivers what we hope for? If we live fighting for control, life becomes consumed with worry. This is a never-ending battle, because even if I were to succeed in controlling my plans on a given day, the day ends and I must work to do it again the next day, and the next. The cycle is endless. The closest thing to complete control that we can know is an illusion. At best, it is a life with little freedom, restricted by micromanagement. And what if it were possible? What if I could live in complete control of my life—if all my plans, thoughts, and actions were predictable—thus eliminating all possibility of pain or failure? Would this bring happiness?

In reality, it isn't control we desire. It is the knowledge that we are perfectly loved and cared for. It is fear that we may not be perfectly loved and cared for that compels us to seek control. Do we trust our Creator to love and care for us perfectly?

The knowledge of good and evil so easily tempts us to trust ourselves rather than God.

If we could learn to relinquish control on a daily basis, we would experience immense joy. Inviting God to be involved in our daily affairs is the most logical thing to do, and the most freeing. Giving God control is easier on some days than others. In general, it is something that we must come back to, over and over again, throughout our day. As we do this, we discover a joy that surpasses anything we have ever known. When we live our lives trying to maintain control, we lose the joy of being dependent upon our all-powerful God. The desire to control our lives is rooted in the fear of missing out on what we want from life. We are afraid that life will not happen according to our plan. This need for control is often how we resist God's loving involvement in our lives and how, ultimately, we miss out on experiencing His best for us. We want control because we are afraid to trust and we tend to doubt God's love. Jesus wants control because He is trustworthy and He loves us.

Control Issues from the Beginning

Our struggle to trust God's plan over our own is nothing new. The very first human beings failed to see God's sovereignty and instead desired control over their lives. The early chapters of the book of Genesis describe the Garden of Eden as a place of unending pleasure for Adam and Eve, a place where they could thoroughly enjoy God's goodness. So long as they lived according to God's intentions, Adam and Eve were blessed to the utmost. Yet, under the influence of the serpent, they began to doubt God's goodness and think obedience to Him would mean missing out on something better.

I have always wondered about this tree in the middle of the Garden of Eden, and why it was called the tree of the "knowledge of good and evil." Knowledge itself, especially knowledge about right and wrong, is good, isn't it? To add to the mystery of this story, it seems that what the serpent said was true. The serpent said to Eve, "For God knows that when you eat of [the fruit from the tree] your eyes will be opened, and you will be like God, knowing good and evil" (Gen. 3:5). That part was apparently true, because the following verses confirm that after eating the fruit, "the eyes of both of them were opened" (v. 7), and they had become "like [God], knowing good and evil" (v. 22).

We exchange reliance upon the love of our Father
for the control afforded by independence.

They received the prized knowledge, but instead of it being the good thing they hoped for, it was harmful to them. It was an exchange, as if acquiring this knowledge would substitute for depending on God Himself. Instead of adding to their lives, this knowledge robbed them of something essential. It is not that the knowledge of good and evil is bad in itself, but when we run first to this knowledge, rather than running to God in our everyday decisions, it becomes a problem. The knowledge of good and evil would equip us to make decisions on our own, to be our own bosses, to become our own gods. Instead of needing our Creator, we could be self-sufficient; we could be in control.

The knowledge of good and evil so easily tempts us to trust ourselves rather than God. When we give into that mindset, it is as though we are eating again from that forbidden tree. We exchange God-centered living for self-centered living. In our effort to take control, we push God out of the picture and we end up missing out on all God has for us. Running to the tree of the knowledge of good and evil robs us of constant fellowship with Jesus.

The message of the serpent is in its nature deceptive but appears to be quite clear—there is an alternative, another way to do life, a way other than what God intended. Today, the enemy speaks the same message, saying, "You can do it on your own. You can do it without God." Just as he convinced Adam and Eve, the enemy somehow convinces us to believe that God does not have our best interests in mind, that God is withholding some good from us, that there is something else that would actually improve and enhance our lives. However, this is not the nature and character of God; He is a good Father, who desires to give us good gifts.

We have thousands of decisions to make every day. A basic knowledge of good and evil allows us to know the difference between right and wrong. It equips us to make our own decisions, but it also gives us a false sense of independence. Instead of running to God with every decision and enjoying close fellowship with Him, we stay right where we are and continue to rely on ourselves. The biggest problem is that we end up missing out on the very thing that we were created for—relationship with God. We exchange reliance upon the love of our Father for the control afforded by independence.

Including God in Everything

From what we see in Scripture, life for Adam and Eve was about fellowship with God. But including God in everything seems tedious to some. We tend to give God control when it comes to "big" decisions, but we still manage the "small" ones. This is actually encouraged by books and by Christians in the church. I think God wants to be involved in every aspect of our lives, no matter how seemingly insignificant. I have found that the more I include God in everything I do, the more I enjoy His fellowship.

The question is: "How much do I want God to be involved in my life?"

When I graduated from high school, like many students, I was faced with the difficult decision of where I should go to college. I had applied to several universities and was finally accepted to three of them. However, I didn't know which of those three would be best, or if there was yet another better option. I remember thinking through my decision very carefully, trying to determine what would be the best choice, the wisest option. I was still unsure of myself, so I asked others what they thought and considered their advice.

Finally, in desperation I decided to include God—what a noble idea! As I did, I immediately felt God speak to me, simply saying, "Listen to your grandmother." I was somewhat surprised but decided right then to bypass all my other considerations and approaches to decision making and to trust this simple impulse. I followed my grandmother's advice and went to Wheaton College. I have never regretted the decision. What did I learn from that decision-making process?

Aside from the fact that I was blessed with a wise grand-mother, the most important thing I learned was that I need to include God in every decision I make. I learned that even my best thinking is not enough, and that opening the door to God's involvement in my decision is essential. I also began to learn about how eager God is to be a part of my journey and how much He is delighted by my requests for help.

It is not that we are incapable of making good decisions; it is about enjoying God's gracious involvement in our lives.

During my time at Wheaton, and ever since, I became more and more convinced that it was the best possible place in the world for me to be in college. It was there that God placed within me a desire to use my degree in business administration as the administrator of an eye hospital in Kabul, Afghanistan. I felt as though God proved the rightness of my college decision to me over and over again, and my association with Wheaton has only brought blessing into my life.

The question is: "How much do I want God to be involved in my life?" Do we want to hear God's input about how we spend our time on the weekend? Will we stop to ask for His ideas about what we should do during our summer holidays? Are we curious about what He wants us to do with the money from our tax return? God wants to be involved in these decisions. He does not want to withhold good from us. He wants to bless us far beyond what we can imagine.

In our limited understanding, we make decisions based on what we want and on what seems best to us. God sees everything in perspective and wants to work things out for our good because He loves us. If we trusted that, we would be more deliberate about including God in our daily routines and pausing regularly to ask for His help, His direction, and His perspective. We may question whether or not God really wants that kind of interaction with us. Maybe we feel we are doing just fine on our own. But it is not that we are incapable of making good decisions; it is about enjoying God's gracious involvement in our lives.

Our lives are ultimately measured not by outward standards of accomplishment but by the inward richness of our fellowship with the Creator.

Sometimes we may think, "I'm doing all right. I'm doing good things. I'm not messing up my life. It doesn't matter how I make decisions, as long as they're good ones." However, we must remember that we live in God's world and for His purposes. Fellowship and communion with our heavenly Father are precisely what we miss out on when we try to take control. Our lives are ultimately measured not by outward standards of accomplishment but by the inward richness of our fellowship with the Creator.

Involving God in our daily decisions does not mean He always gives clear direction. Sometimes He says nothing, and sometimes He says, "Do what you want." The treasure is the conversation, journey, and collaboration. Trusting does not mean putting your hope in God for a specific answer, outcome, or even "right" decision. Trusting means maintaining confidence in the character of God and believing that His goodness, mercy, and loving-kindness will pursue and overtake us at all times.

It is important to understand that this desire we have to take control of our lives is extremely dangerous. It has the potential to destroy what is most precious within us—our simple faith and trust in God. We need to understand that, ultimately, we do not always know what is best for us, and, as much as we want to be in control and make bold attempts to assert our independence, we are not in control. God is! If we struggle with control issues—which we all do in some way—it always begins with believing less about God. If we do not have full faith in God's goodness and unconditional love, we do not completely trust Him with our lives. We are content to have God involved in the little bits of our lives we are comfortable with—we can trust that much. But God is sovereign, and when we can learn to trust Him and His way, we will find that it is truly a beautiful way.

God is greater than we know, and when things spin out of control, it is actually a wonderful invitation to run to Him.

It is not an uncommon reaction to our daily lives to seek a semblance of control in what areas we can. Perhaps when our studies, work, home life, or relationships become overwhelming, we escape to food, shopping, sports, video games, social distractions, or some other form of indulgence, where our own actions give us immediate satisfaction. We go to the places where we call the shots, where we pull the strings, and where our desires are fulfilled without obstacles.

For some, the need to feel in control goes beyond the times when we feel overwhelmed. I have heard people say, often jokingly, "Oh, I'm a bit of a control freak." People can say this quite flippantly. I wonder if we could look at this a bit more seriously for a moment. Could it be that the heart behind being controlling actually robs us of intimacy with God? The reality is that God is greater than we know, and when things spin out of control, it is actually a wonderful invitation to run to God and discover His ability to completely satisfy us in that moment.

I think people often misunderstand the issue of control. It is always a matter of the heart and our motives, which means that unhealthy control can be difficult to detect simply by looking at someone's actions. I believe that God has gifted people differently. Some people are wired to pay attention to details in ways that others are not, but that does not necessarily make them overly desirous of control. Some administrators are gifted in organization. Some accountants really do love keeping accurate track of numbers and finances. Some gardeners find great joy in planting flowers or vegetables in perfect configurations. Some writers take pleasure in crafting sentences and correcting punctuation. All of these talents and abilities are wonderful things, but we miss out when we use our gifts as an attempt to control the people and circumstances that come into our lives without inviting God's involvement.

---

*I decided to trust His character despite
the fear I felt in my heart.*

God cares about each one of us and about every detail of our lives. He cares about changing diapers, about math homework, about baseball practice, about lunch, about the flat tire on your car, and about your choosing the color of the curtains in your living room. He wants to be included in these areas of your life! He wants to set us free so we can trust Him completely and enjoy our relationship with Him. He wants things to work out for us according to His perfect plan and in His perfect time. We simply need to trust in His goodness. There truly is no better alternative than for God to be involved in every aspect of our lives.

The important thing is that we learn to trust. When we struggle with control, we need to take very practical steps to exercise trust and let God show us new ways of doing things. We are often tempted to take control, and we need to respond by trusting Jesus. We need to surrender our way and allow God to have His way and trust that it is better! Oftentimes, God brings change into our lives to give us the opportunity to place our lives in His hands. We do not need to fear the loss of what we surrender; He only wants us to cling to Him more and to enjoy true safety and security in Him.

Learning to Trust

Just before I was imprisoned in Iran, I was faced with a decision that tested my trust in God, a time when I sought to gain control for myself. After our passports were confiscated at the border and Glenn and I were told to return Tehran, Iran's capital, for questioning, we were granted three days before our appointment. We returned to our host's house, and he graciously offered to let us stay with him for the additional days. On one of those days, he took us for a scenic drive along the Iran-Turkmenistan border. I took notice of the miles of fencing separating the two countries and saw that they were left unguarded by soldiers. I had a thought: I could climb that fence to freedom and escape Iran. I could deal with the consequences in Turkmenistan, which would undoubtedly be less severe than the problems I might face in Iran. Should I flee the country?

There was no doubt in my mind—I wanted to leave! What I really wanted was to be in control of the situation, especially in the midst of all the uncertainty and fear about what would happen when I got to Tehran. I tried to justify my desire and even spiritualize it. "Maybe God is giving me a way out, providing an easy escape." I tried to hope that it was true, but I knew in my heart that God wanted me to stay, and I chose to accept His will. I chose His way instead of what seemed to be the wiser and safer way. I surrendered.

Even when I feel afraid and the
fear feels overwhelming, I can still
walk forward trusting Him.

On another occasion, a year after my imprisonment, I had the clear sense that God was calling me to serve Him again in Central Asia, this time in Ashgabat, Turkmenistan. I was afraid to go. I struggled with the idea of being in that part of the world again with the risks that it involved. I knew that if I did not go, I was avoiding the obvious call on my life. I wanted to trust God, but I was afraid that He might not take care of me. Eventually, I went. I decided to trust His character despite the fear I felt in my heart.

I went to Turkmenistan on a student visa that had to be renewed monthly in a government office. Every time I thought about going into one of these offices, I was overcome by fear. I was reminded about my torture in Iran and was afraid the same thing would happen again. The first time I went to renew my visa, I saw that the building was the former headquarters of the KGB. Suddenly, it all felt too familiar. Fear came over my soul. I looked to God and felt His nudging to walk forward.

Despite my building anxiety, I knew I could trust God, no matter what was about to happen to me. As I entered the building and presented my paperwork, I was ushered into a private room in the back. All I could think about was my experience in Iran. Was I heading back to prison? I wanted to take control of the situation, leave the country, and find another way to get a visa. But I knew I could not run. So instead, I ran to God and pleaded for His help.

I sat down at a table facing two men. "Why do you want to stay in our country?" one of them asked in English. I replied simply, "Because I want to learn Russian and help your people." Instantly he replied, with a smile on his face, "Okay, here's your extension." I could not believe it! My heart was flooded with joy and relief. I thanked God for His faithfulness. I began to realize that even when I feel afraid and the fear feels overwhelming, I can still walk forward trusting Him. The seemingly paralyzing effects of fear are truly not as strong or powerful as God's love.

The most responsible thing to do in every situation is to run to God and do what He says!

My older sister experienced something similar years ago, while serving as a missionary in Nepal. After two years, she and several local believers were imprisoned for sharing the gospel. She was released on bail after nine days. She then faced a three-year probation period, wherein she had to appear before the Nepali court every month as it reevaluated her case. She knew that every time she stood before the judge, there was a chance she could be put back in prison. She could have left the country, but what she chose to do was run to God. This is what He said: "Stay in the country and associate yourself with the persecution of the local believers who don't have the choice to run." She did and remained there, becoming part of the story that God is writing in Nepal.

The Bible teaches us that obedience to God can bring us into conflict and difficulties and, sometimes, pain. The rewards of obedience and faithfulness far outweigh the effects of any obstacles that come into our path. In fact, even the obstacles turn into opportunities to learn and grow in our faith. That is why James can write, "When troubles of any kind come your way, consider it an opportunity for great joy" (James 1:2 NLT). Likewise, Paul writes, "Our present troubles are small and won't last very long. Yet they produce for us a glory that vastly outweighs them and will last forever" (2 Cor. 4:17 NLT). I am not saying that we should seek out pain and difficulty or that we should search for trials in our lives. I am saying that when trials come, we should run to God and obey His leading.

Wisdom and Responsibility

Some people would say that the most responsible thing for me and Glenn to do in our situation in Iran would have been to leave the country and find another way. The most responsible thing to do in every situation is to run to God and do what He says! In so doing, we may encounter risk that seems painful or difficult, but it is worth it! Giving God control and letting Him have the final say means bringing our concerns to Jesus in constant communion. We need to learn the lifestyle of Proverbs 3:5–6: "Trust God from the bottom of your heart; don't try to figure out everything on your own. Listen for God's voice in everything you do, everywhere you go; he's the one who will keep you on track" (*The Message*).

Sometimes we do things we call common sense or wisdom in order to run from things we are actually afraid of, so as to maintain a sense of control. For example, when a high school graduate is faced with the question of college, what should she do? I know people who automatically assume that you must go to college after high school; it is common sense, the wisest thing to do. But is it always? Jesus invites us to run to Him and ask. In my own family, my parents sought God about what each of their children should do after high school. My older sister felt led to join YWAM, and my parents blessed that. I can see clearly, from the fruit in her life, that this was the wisest thing for her to do. She has never been to college.

Oftentimes, letting go of our own expectations is just not easy. We are afraid of change—we fear the unknown. "What if God asks me to move to Africa or tells me to quit my job—will He keep me safe? What if He asks me to fast or to give more than I am comfortable giving—will He provide? What if He asks me to give up my Saturday to serve a neighbor—will He meet my need?" The list of fears is endless. Yet, when we allow these questions to keep us from trusting Him, that is when our understanding of God is too small; we have forgotten His heart and we need to ask God to reveal Himself to us. In my journey, the knowledge of God and my fellowship with Him have been the greatest treasures of my life—they are worth everything.

Sometimes trusting God is easy,
and sometimes it is not.

People say to me, "Okay, Dan, I can surrender my life to God, but what about my kids' lives? You don't have children, so you don't know how hard it is to give up control of them." True, I do not have children of my own, but I do know that God, as their heavenly Father, has a plan for them that is more perfect than any earthly parent's could be. When my friends ask me about this, I certainly do not know what that plan entails—I only talk about the deep love and concern that Jesus has for their children. God's plan looks different for every family and for every child. My heart leaps with excitement every time I think about all the plans Jesus has for this next generation.

The wisest decision ever made was the Father sending His Son into the world to die for us, even though it put Jesus on the path of fear and risk.

Sometimes trusting God is easy, and sometimes it is not. Does God's will for our lives sometimes appear less attractive than other options we may be considering? Certainly. But in the end, God's way is the best. When I was standing in Iran, on the border of Turkmenistan, I was so tempted to hop the fence, to plan my own escape. Instead, I listened to that gentle nudging in my heart that said, "Stay." In hindsight, although my experience was horrific, I am grateful that I did what I felt I was supposed to do. For all the pain I endured, I have no regrets about it, because I know I was obeying God's leading. My fellowship with God grew through my experience, and there is nothing better than being nearer to Him.

True wisdom always invites us to follow God wholeheartedly. Abraham made a wise choice when he decided to take the risk of leaving everything in order to obey God. Peter made a wise choice when he stepped out of the boat and into the waves to join Jesus on the water. The wisest decision ever made was the Father sending His Son into the world to die for us, even though it put Jesus on the path of fear and risk. Taking risks is part of God's character, and as we walk in obedience to Him, we will find the risks we encounter are actually an acceptable part of His plan for our lives.

There is nothing more life-giving than following God's leading. Romans 8:28 tells us that God is working out all things "for the good of those who love him, who have been called according to his purpose." Stacked against all our common sense and any other human wisdom, nothing is wiser than trusting in God. When we discover the love of the Father and His plan for us, the fear of losing control loses its influence over our hearts. The God of the universe has adopted us, and His love is immense! The more I rest in the reality that God is a good and loving Father, and the more I trust Him, the more the stress of the unknown loses its grip on my life. I can trust God because I am completely His and nothing will ever change that.

Jesus gave up total control of His life and "for the joy set before him endured" all things (Heb. 12:2). He invites us to do the same and, in so doing, fully enjoy everything He has for us. Jesus wants to be a part of everything. He really does, because He loves you. Jesus wants desperately to be in control of your life, because He alone knows what is best for you. If you thought right now about what a perfect day could look like—down to the smallest detail—do you know that it still would not be as good as what God intends for you? Do you believe that about God? Truly, God wants to show us a better way and bless us with more than we can imagine.

Jesus, thank You that You have everything in control. Help me to surrender my life to You and allow You to take control. Help me give You my fear of losing control. Give me a deeper revelation of Your goodness. I know that You have good things in store for me and that You always have my best in mind. Help me today to begin to trust You more and to embrace the life that You are calling me to live. Amen.

chapter four

Fear and Finances

When it comes to fear, financial security is usually
near the top of the list. Money is a strong influence in today's world, and there are many fears related to our
finances. Everywhere I travel and teach, I encounter people
who are worried about their financial needs. Over the past
thirty years, I have grown to love God's involvement in my
financial matters. I have had times of need, when I did not
know how I could survive with such limited means, and I
have had times of being blessed far beyond what I needed.
Through all this, I discovered that money should not be our
main concern. The joy of life, in having much or having little,
is in including God in the journey and trusting Him to provide along the way.

The Bible has a great deal to say about money. I want
to highlight several biblical attitudes, which are critical for
us today as we think about finances. God does not want our
financial concerns to rule our lives or to be a source of fear

and anxiety. He wants finances to be an area of blessing in our lives, where we see Him meet our every need.

Security in Jesus

What happens when we feel we have lost our financial security? Do we find there is more stress in our home? Do we find ourselves more argumentative with our spouse or roommate; do we lose sleep; do we immediately cut back on the children's allowance; do we cancel our family vacation that was planned months ago; do we stop tithing? We make great sacrifices to become financially secure, and yet it seems we never have enough. Some people live their lives as though they need money more than anything else, even more than God. We must realize, in the midst of these concerns, that we have an invitation to run to God. We desperately need His perspective.

We make great sacrifices to become financially secure, and yet it seems we never have enough.

The Bible is full of warnings about how the love of money can twist our thinking and lead us astray. The words of Jesus are clear: "Do not store up for yourselves treasures on earth. . . . For where your treasure is, there your heart will be also. . . . You cannot serve both God and Money" (Matt. 6:19, 21, 24). God is most concerned about our hearts. A strong pressure within our society feeds an impulse in our hearts to store up treasures on earth. We want to be free to serve God, but the worldview that "you have to have money to survive" and "the more money, the better" screams loudly that it is impossible to live only to serve God.

We often make decisions based on financial resources rather than on the command of God. We know that money is not everything, yet it seems easier to put our trust in money rather than in God. One thing I am sure of is this: Jesus can provide for us and give us great joy in ways that money never could and was never intended to. Just as with our desires for the absence of fear and for control, something deeper underlies our desire for financial security. At its core, the desire for financial security is a desire to be at peace and know that everything is taken care of. The hard truth is that money was never supposed to be the thing we turn to for this assurance. Jesus is our one and only security.

Trusting God

My heart for others is that they would be set free from their financial fears. I want to see people walking by faith and trusting God to take care of their needs. I love the simplicity of Jesus's message on money in the Sermon on the Mount. He addresses our practical concerns about how we are going to afford food and clothing. We worry so much about these things, but Jesus keeps pointing us back to how much our Father in heaven cares about us. If we are focused on God, then God will make sure we have what we need. Jesus says, "Seek first his kingdom and his righteousness, and all these things will be given to you as well" (Matt. 6:33).

What does it look like to seek first His kingdom and righteousness? It means always including God and asking Him what to do with our daily decisions, knowing we will be given what He knows we need. Oftentimes, securing basic necessities—as well as our desire for more than these—becomes the foundation and fuel for our decision making. Nevertheless, we can trust God; He will provide for us. Do we truly believe that?

About eight years ago, just before the real estate collapse in America, I felt led by God to invest in property in southern Utah. The guidance was clear and came with confirmations over many months. With much excitement and anticipation, I purchased the land. Over the next few years, the value of the land crashed; I lost tens of thousands of dollars. I was angry and very frustrated, not just at myself, but also at God, because I felt He had led me to invest.

Money can never replace the joy and
security we find in the love of God.

What was really going on in my heart? After all, I had enough food to eat and I had enough money to take care of my daily needs. The problem was that I began to doubt all the instances in which I felt God's direction. Would He prompt me into such a failed investment, and if so, why would He do that to me? My heart had been exposed—I did not fully trust God.

The anger I was experiencing exposed my lack of trust. I needed to repent. I asked God to purify my heart and was filled with a deep peace. I chose to believe that God would continue to provide for all my needs. I could be wrong, but I do think God led me to invest the money, knowing I would lose it, with the intention of refining my heart and character. In hindsight, I feel my fellowship with Jesus grew to a deeper place; this experience became yet another testimony to God's ongoing work in my life to make me more like Jesus.

It is very interesting to me that Jesus tells us, "You cannot serve both God and Money" (Matt. 6:24). In our hearts, we must be loyal to either one or the other. As I travel around the world, it is evident that the greatest obstacle to people seeking first the kingdom of God is the temptation to let money run their lives. God wants to direct our lives. He does not want our fears and anxieties about money to influence our decisions to obey Him. Yet I have talked to many people who find it incredibly difficult to bring God into the realm of their finances.

This is it! Knowing Jesus is everything.

We devote so much time and energy to earning, saving, and spending money, and it is sometimes difficult to know how to include God in all these activities. It may or may not come easily to trust God with what we should give Him out of our earnings; however, it can be even more difficult to know how to include Him in our daily expenditures. According to the Bible, how we consider money reveals some aspect of where our hearts are. God wants to be involved in this part of our lives, not because He wants us to live without money or with limited means, but because He wants to give us a non-dependent perspective on money. Money can never replace the joy and security we find in the love of God.

Setting Fear Aside

What is it we are afraid of? Some are afraid of not having enough money, while others are afraid of not managing their money well. We are afraid of the ups and downs of our financial circumstances. When we have too little, we are afraid of the difficulties that want brings. When we have more than we need, we are afraid of the responsibilities that plenty brings. While these concerns are legitimate, I believe an issue of contentment is behind them. The apostle Paul shares his thoughts when he writes to the Philippians, "I have learned to be content whatever the circumstances. I know what it is to be in need, and I know what it is to have plenty. I have learned the secret of being content in any and every situation, whether well fed or hungry, whether living in plenty or in want. I can do everything through him who gives me strength" (Phil. 4:11–13). How did Paul do it?

If you were offered a hundred million dollars or a relationship with Jesus, which would you choose?

A few days into my imprisonment, the guards gave me back my Bible. I spent the weeks reading, and I discovered a deep revelation of Paul's heart. More than any book, I dove into Philippians and learned that Paul was not only content with any situation but also joyful in all things. How could Paul write a book about joy and contentment while sitting in prison? I must have read through Philippians more than thirty times, desperately searching for the key to Paul's contentment. I wanted that! I think I found an answer in Philippians 3:7–8, where Paul says, "I once thought these things were valuable, but now I consider them worthless because of what Christ has done. Yes, everything else is worthless when compared with the infinite value of knowing Christ Jesus my Lord. For his sake I have discarded everything else, counting it all as garbage, so that I could gain Christ" (NLT).

This is it! Knowing Jesus is everything. Whether or not he had freedom, comfort, friends, or money, Paul was content because he had Jesus! Not only was he content, but he was so convinced of God's love, and the joy it brought him, that he could write a book about joy while wasting away in prison. Paul did not have money—he did not have anything. Yet he found true contentment with Christ in his life.

Do you know what it is to be in financial need? Do you know what it is to have plenty? Neither circumstance is more godly than the other. If you were offered a hundred million dollars or a relationship with Jesus, which would you choose? To be honest, the money sounds enticing to me! But would I choose it over the insurmountable riches of walking with Jesus in relationship every day? I have never been offered this kind of money, but, like Paul, I am learning and discovering that Jesus is worth a great deal more.

Our fears about finances are an invitation to discover God's commitment to provide for us.

Freedom

We can be free of worry, free of guilt, and free of the fear of having too much or too little. Wealth does not need to rule our hearts or control us, whatever our financial situation. We can live in freedom. God wants to give us freedom in our finances. God wants to set our hearts free so we can say, "I can handle poverty. I can handle wealth. I'll be content with whatever You give me." How do we come to that kind of freedom? Most of us think that when we have enough money, we will stop worrying about it. John D. Rockefeller was once asked how much money he thought would be enough. He replied, "Just a little bit more." However, our freedom, security, and survival are not found in our bank accounts; they are found in our relationship with Jesus. Our fears about finances are an invitation to discover God's commitment to provide for us.

I have been incredibly blessed to have positive role models who walk in integrity with their finances. One of the greatest examples for me has been Loren Cunningham, the founder of YWAM. Early in life, Loren had opportunities to inherit a large sum of money and pursue a life in business. However, he gave up his rights to wealth and chose a simple lifestyle of trust and obedience to Jesus. Loren single-mindedly pursued the call of God, despite financial obstacles. Throughout his life, he has had times of great financial blessing and times of financial need. I have had the privilege of traveling with Loren on several occasions and have been thoroughly impressed with his generosity and freedom from financial concern. He simply makes Jesus the focal point of his life.

True financial freedom is simply doing what God wants you to do with your money.

My parents also modeled a lifestyle of focusing on Jesus more than money. For most of their lives, they were led to give away 30 percent of their gross income. Although it meant some amount of sacrifice for our family, obeying Jesus in this brought great joy and contentment. My parents always pointed my siblings and me to Jesus and instructed us to simply do whatever He said to do, no matter what the price tag was. Even when it appeared finances were not available, they never discouraged us from obeying what we felt God was telling us. As I seek to follow these role models in my life, I am enjoying the fruit and freedom of focusing on Jesus and not allowing money to control me.

If we are holding twenty dollars in our hand, maybe we need to ask, "God, what should I do with this?" We may give it away to someone else, we may buy lunch with it, or we may just put it back in our pocket. Whatever we do, it is important that we know in our hearts that the money belongs to God. We only need to be obedient to Him with it. We can make our financial decisions without fear. When we obey God, we can give money away without being afraid that we will not have enough for our needs. We can spend it on ourselves without feeling shame. We can save it without feeling guilt. The point is not what we do with our money. The point is to be free. True financial freedom is simply doing what God wants you to do with your money.

Openness

As I counsel people, I see a lot of guilt and shame connected to money matters. People are often very private when it comes to how they spend their money, even though the Bible talks openly about it. We are willing to be open and vulnerable about other areas of our lives, but we put our walls up whenever the topic of finances surfaces. Why is it that we are encouraged to be so open to accountability in other areas of moral conduct or devotional life but not in how much we pay for rent, what we spend our paycheck on, or how much we give away? Why do we often feel embarrassed, even scared, to talk about finances?

I have seen wonderful fruit come from living in openness with financial matters. When nothing is closed or hidden, it has actually helped me to walk in the light and live free from the fear and love of money. What does it mean to walk in this kind of openness? It does not mean that it is necessary for someone else to approve every financial decision; we are encouraged to follow the Holy Spirit in every decision of life.

Ultimately, I think we are supposed to make our own decisions with our money. However, accountability will help us grow as financial stewards.

Financial openness is not about creating a set of rules; it is about creating a community that fosters an attitude toward money that is rooted in simple obedience to Jesus. Perhaps, when it comes to large investments or expenditures, we sometimes need to consider the counsel of others. Perhaps, like me, you would benefit from inviting a group of friends to speak directly into your financial affairs at any time. As followers of Jesus, we need to include others in our financial journey.

Having generosity means being fearlessly concerned with blessing others as God directs rather than focusing on our own needs and wants.

Some people say, "I shouldn't include other people in my financial matters because the Bible says, 'When you give to the needy, do not let your left hand know what your right hand is doing'" (Matt. 6:3). However, they are misrepresenting Jesus's words. Jesus is addressing those who are making a public show of their giving, in order to be applauded by others. It was not openness that Jesus was critiquing, but the motives of the heart. Moreover, it is clear in Acts, and throughout the New Testament, that financial openness was a healthy part of the lifestyle of the apostles and believers. Jesus praised Mary's display of extravagance when she poured out perfume, worth a year's wages, on his feet (John 12:1–8). Barnabas publicly shared his wealth to encourage and strengthen the work of the early church (Acts 4:36–37). Jesus also commended the widow who publicly gave her mite as an offering (Luke 21:1–4).

The Scriptures encourage us to walk in the light, meaning that we ought to live our lives in openness and integrity: "If we are living in the light, as God is in the light, then we have fellowship with each other" (1 John 1:7 NLT). When things are in the light, they are visible. When they are visible, they are known for what they are.

As we walk in the light, together with others, we need to be careful to avoid being judgmental. "Why did they spend their money like that? Why didn't they spend their money like this?" I have had these thoughts myself. We need to seek to trust our brothers and sisters regarding how they spend, or do not spend, their money. I see a lot of unnecessary criticism in this area. It is easy to judge, but how can we know what is in their hearts or what God has asked of them?

As we walk in simple obedience and do our best to be faithful, we need to trust that others are doing the same. Jesus came as the light, to show us the Father and to show us how to live. The words of Jesus are so clear: "Do not judge, or you too will be judged" (Matt. 7:1). If we value the freedom and grace that we have in Jesus, then we will extend that freedom and grace to others both within our community and throughout the world. This, in turn, will make it easier for us to be open with one another about our finances.

Generosity

The New Testament clearly emphasizes generosity. Having generosity means being fearlessly concerned with blessing others as God directs rather than focusing on our own needs and wants. Again, the story in John 12 in which Mary anoints Jesus has a lot to say about generosity and about our attitudes toward money and each other. Jesus is having dinner with some of His friends, including Lazarus, the man He raised from the dead not long before. While Martha is serving

the meal, Mary pulls out a jar of expensive perfume and pro-
ceeds to pour it out on Jesus's feet and then dries His feet
with her hair. The extravagance of her act of love is obvious;
she is holding nothing back in her display of gratitude and
devotion to Jesus. To her, Jesus is worth the extravagance, no
matter how much she spent in her effort. The fact that the
perfume was worth about one year's salary did not deter her.
She seems to disregard the price, with care only for the person
she is honoring. It seems there is something about money that
is connected to our hearts, and God is very interested in this.

---

*The more I involve Jesus in every financial decision,
the more I discover it is always for my good.*

Does our love for Jesus look like Mary's? Are we willing
to let our acts of generosity be this extravagant? Mary's generosity should challenge us because Jesus is worthy of such
extravagance. Not only is He worthy of our extravagance,
but also He occasionally leads us to spend in ways that seem
extravagant to accomplish His blessing. When I was living in
Afghanistan, I received a letter from a close friend in Australia
inviting me to be the best man in his wedding. I was honored
by his invitation, but I immediately thought that it would be
far too expensive to fly to Australia for a wedding. I wrote my
friend back and expressed my regret about not being able to
attend. However, I felt very uneasy about the decision over the
next few days. I decided to pray about it, and as I did, I felt an
immediate peace and urging from God to make plans to be at
the wedding in Australia. The only problem was that I did not
have the money to buy the ticket. As I looked at my finances,
I saw I had only enough money to get a round-trip ticket to

Bangkok, Thailand. Even though it seemed crazy, I decided to take that first step and see what would happen from there.

If you are doing what you feel God is leading you to do, then by definition you are living by faith.

After arriving in Bangkok, I called my family and asked them to pray. My mother prayed and felt that she was to lend me the money for the ticket to Australia, as long as I would pay it back within a month. I went ahead and purchased the ticket for $825. At the wedding, I was asked about my work in Afghanistan and then invited to speak at two different gatherings. At both of these places, people approached me wanting to contribute toward my financial support. Later that week, when I boarded the plane back to Bangkok, I had $820 to pay back my mother. After I told her the story, she said I could keep the remaining five dollars!

If we are able to respond openly to God with our finances, then we need not worry about what happens beyond our simple obedience, even if we suffer some kind of loss. Jesus invites us to a simple life of trusting Him and obeying everything He tells us to do. We can leave the results in His loving hands with freedom and contentment in our hearts. This option is far better than always trying to keep things within our own grasp. A life of simple obedience includes every financial decision we make. The more I involve Jesus in every financial decision, the more I discover it is always for my good.

Living by Faith

Another area we need to rethink in relation to finances is our use of the phrase "living by faith." These words are often

used to describe someone who works in a church, or a minis-
try-related organization, and whose income depends upon the
gifts of others' donations. Yet this is not a strict example of
what "living by faith" means. Living by faith is not another
category of our spiritual life; it is nothing other than simple
obedience. It does not belong only in the lives of missionaries
and pastors—all believers are called to live by faith. Simply
put, if you are doing what you feel God is leading you to do,
then by definition you are living by faith, whether you are a
banker, pastor, plumber, missionary, or schoolteacher.

---

*Jesus invites us into hope and freedom and
promises He will always take care of us.
This is the most secure and trustworthy
economic advice we could ever get.*

Sometimes our circumstances demand a great deal of faith.
Even so, there is one thing that dictates hope for our financial future: God's faithfulness. We are surrounded by financial need every day. It is in our neighborhoods and churches
and portrayed in the media on a local, national, and global
scale. We hear how unstable the economy is and how vulnerable we are. Despite this, we must live in faith, believing in
God's provision. Will He really be able to take care of us? The
answer is an overwhelming yes! Economic risks are inevitable
in our world today, but I have learned that they are simply
opportunities to run to God and live out my simple faith and
trust in Him. When we give our ears and hearts to too much
talk about economic disaster, we give fear a foothold in our
lives. We forfeit the joy and freedom God is offering us. Jesus

invites us into hope and freedom and promises He will always take care of us. This is the most secure and trustworthy economic advice we could ever get.

Again, we need to realize that God uses our finances—incomes, spending, and giving—to get at our hearts. When we struggle financially and become afraid and anxious, our hearts are exposed. That vulnerable place is an invitation to deeper intimacy and deeper trust. God not only wants to provide for us; He also wants to set our hearts free. When it comes to our practices and patterns of giving, it is important to remember that all that we have belongs to God and that He wants us to be generous as He is generous. I believe it is important to be free to respond to the promptings in our hearts. If we give generously out of a sense of God's leading, then we have found freedom in our finances.

When it comes right down to it, the only acceptable way to deal with our money is to trust and obey God. God wants to lead us. He has our best interests in mind. He wants to bless us through a lifestyle of openness and generosity when it comes to our resources. Our best option is always to let God take control. We need to give Him our fears, open our hearts, and commit all our possessions to Him. He invites us to invite Him into all the financial decisions we make. When we do, we will find that it is, by far, the best way to live.

Jesus, thank You for Your promise to take care of my every need. Help me to trust You with my finances. Help me to be more open with others about my finances and generous with what You have given me. I want my resources to be a blessing to others. Help me rest in the knowledge that You will take care of all my needs. Thank You for the freedom You offer. Amen.

chapter five

Risky Obedience

R isk is an integral part of the human experience. We all take risks, from our very first steps as toddlers to every time we get into a vehicle. We will never be able to escape risk in this life. Of course, there is wisdom in being alert and cautious—we look both ways before crossing the street; we have a healthy fear of speeding in vehicles; we learn not to play with fire; we learn to respect things like deep water and wild animals and to obey signs that read "Stop," "Do Not Touch," or "Mind the Gap." But sometimes we feel caution is not enough. Sometimes we would like to avoid risk altogether. We want a guarantee that nothing bad is going to happen.

Yet the life of faith is full of risks. Jesus never promises us a life free from danger and uncertainty. Following Jesus does not eliminate danger—but it does change the meaning of risk. The more we gaze on Jesus and become enamored by His beauty, the more everything else fades away. We realize that there are risks, but more importantly, there is Jesus. As this reality sets in, the risks we take become less significant and less threatening.

Our faith in God makes a difference in how we manage risk and address safety concerns. Ultimately, our trust in God is at the core of finding our way through fears of uncertainty and harm. We choose to obey, despite the risks, knowing that God loves us and that He has promised to take care of us. Trusting Him gives us a sense of peace and purpose in the midst of danger. We are never alone; God is watching over us with a compassionate concern, like that of a parent for a child.

The words of Psalm 121 have been a comfort to me through many dangerous situations: "The Lord watches over you—the Lord is your shade at your right hand; the sun will not harm you by day, nor the moon by night. The Lord will keep you from all harm—he will watch over your life; the Lord will watch over your coming and going both now and forevermore" (Ps. 121:5–8).

We choose to obey, despite the risks,
knowing that God loves us and that
He has promised to take care of us.

At times, it is hard to reconcile these words with our experiences. When we read that God will keep us from "all harm," we know that it cannot mean we will never encounter danger and difficulty in our lives. We know we are just as susceptible to being injured in a car accident, or developing cancer, as those who do not believe in God. Believers not only experience hardship in their journeys with God; they also are vulnerable to fear of potential danger. Often this fear is the greater challenge. Our faith is not an impenetrable barrier against these things. The difference is that our faith in God's love and presence places us entirely in His control.

My faith in Jesus has made all the difference in the many trials and fears I have faced in my life.

While working at a medical clinic in Afghanistan, I was exposed to and contracted hepatitis. However, it was not until I was back in America for a visit that I began to show symptoms of the disease. The disease has a long incubation period before you actually feel ill, and my doctor was shocked at the advanced stage of the disease. He said it was the worst case of hepatitis he had ever seen. In fact, he was not shy, nor very sensitive, in saying that he had treated people with much milder cases who had succumbed to the disease and died. I was overwhelmed with the reality that in a relatively short time I could die. When I got back to my house, I went to my bedroom and wept as I realized the significance of what the doctor had said. How is it possible that I may only live a few more weeks? I am never going to get married or have a family of my own! Depression quickly set in.

Later that evening, my mom and my sister came into my room to pray for me. When they left, I drifted off to sleep, exhausted. I felt better in the morning, and over the next three weeks I got better and better. My doctor was completely amazed, because he did not even think I had a chance. I was totally healed of hepatitis—Jesus had healed me! Upon my full recovery, I decided to return to Afghanistan and continue the work God had for me there.

Was it risky to go to Afghanistan in the first place? Was it risky to go back after I had just contracted hepatitis? Of course, but concern for my health was not my primary focus. When I first went to Afghanistan, doing what Jesus asked of me was at the center of my focus, and that remained true when I returned after my bout with hepatitis.

Another time, while living in Afghanistan, I walked out of the eye hospital where I worked to run errands in town. As I got into my car, instead of sitting next to my driver, which was my normal practice, I got into the backseat and shut the door. As soon as I sat down, I felt the Spirit prompt me to move to the front seat instead. Is this from me or from God? Why does it matter where I sit? As I wrestled with this question, I prayed and again felt God's gentle nudging to sit up front. I got out and moved up next to the driver.

My life had been miraculously spared.

About ten minutes later, as we drove through the streets of Kabul on our way to town, a sniper, hiding in an apartment building, fired three shots at the vehicle. The bullets ripped right into the backseat where I had been sitting only minutes earlier. I sat in complete shock as we drove beyond the range of the sniper. I was so overwhelmed by what had just happened that I had to ask the driver to pull over. Was it mere coincidence? I do not think so. My life had been miraculously spared.

A few years ago, I visited my younger sister in New Delhi, India. Although I was feeling the effects of jet lag the morning after I arrived, I went out to buy some milk. Since I had visited her neighborhood several times before, the streets were quite familiar to me. Making my way directly to the store, I ran across one lane of traffic and stopped on the concrete median before quickly looking to my right, to make sure the next lane was also free of oncoming traffic. Seeing nothing, I took a step forward and was suddenly stopped in my tracks. I looked down and saw that my left arm was tangled in the fencing along the median.

Just then, a large city bus came rushing by from my left. There is no way the vehicle could have stopped in time had I taken one more step forward. I would have been instantly killed. In my grogginess, I had looked the wrong way, forgetting that cars in India drive on the side opposite of those in North America. I should have died! I had no idea how my arm got caught in the fencing. I stayed on the median for quite a while and held the fence tightly as my body shook. God had spared my life again.

In each of these experiences, God proved to me that He is faithful, good, and more than able to protect me. When I was at risk of dying from hepatitis, I cried out to God, and He healed me. When I was facing risk in Afghanistan because of obedience to Him, He saved me. Sometimes God protects me by telling me what to do, as He did in Afghanistan. Sometimes He supersedes my mind altogether and sovereignly saves me, as He did in New Delhi. Each of these experiences made me more aware of the presence and protection of God in my life. He is worthy of my obedience in taking risks!

Post-Victory Fear

Sometimes, right after seeing God do mighty things and feeling like I can take on the world, I suddenly find myself becoming irrationally fearful and depressed. I know I am not the only one. The Bible tells just such a story in 1 Kings 19. I love this story because it shows Elijah, one of the most amazing men of God in the Scriptures, becoming desperately weak and afraid for his safety, right after a huge victory.

In the previous chapter, Elijah orchestrates an incredible showdown between himself and the 450 prophets of Baal. Elijah stands up before King Ahab of Israel and his wicked wife, Jezebel, and, in an act of courage and faith, witnesses God defeat them. But in the very next chapter, when he hears that

Jezebel wants him killed, he becomes "afraid and [runs] for his life" (v. 3).

After boldly standing up to hundreds of false prophets and witnessing the might of God, Elijah faces one crazy queen and flees! The Bible goes on to say that after running into the wilderness, Elijah sits down under a tree and prays that he might die: "I have had enough, Lord. . . . Take my life" (v. 4).

Have you ever experienced this? Have you ever been at the height of victory and faith, only to come crashing down the next minute and find yourself depressed and afraid of things that were previously insignificant? These fears are irrational, but in the midst of life they feel very real. Our hope is that Jesus comes through for us, not only in times of great faith, but also in times of despair.

Just a few years ago, my friend and I decided to go on a mission trip to Nigeria. After weeks of prayer, we felt God directing us to go and provide all our own finances. In the process, we were given twenty to thirty words of knowledge as confirmation that we were to make this trip. Once our visas had been promised by the Nigerian embassy in Washington, DC, we bought our tickets. The day before we were supposed to receive our visas, however, a man from the Nigerian embassy called me and told me our visas had been denied. I freaked out, right over the phone. I reminded him that the visas had already been promised to us. But without another word, he hung up.

I could not sleep the whole night. God had told us to go, He had provided all the money, and He had given multiple words of encouragement through our friends. We were all set to go, but in one little moment it all went down the drain. Where was God? Why did this happen? I paced in my room until 6:00 a.m. and finally decided to pray. Immediately, I felt God ask me a question.

"Why are you so worried?"

"Because the embassy denied our visas and told us we can't go!"

"Call them back tomorrow."

An hour later, I got on the phone and the same man I had talked to the night before answered. He said, "Have a wonderful time in Nigeria. I've overnighted your visas and passports to your address."

We ought to come alongside each other with compassionate concern, not minimizing another's fears with criticism or condemnation.

I was stunned by God's goodness. I had spent the whole night worrying, only to receive a blessing in the morning. Like Elijah, I went straight from experiencing a spiritual high to being very weak and afraid, allowing my focus to be on the circumstances and not on Jesus.

Why do we do this? Why, after experiencing God's power in incredible ways, do we so often crash and sink into hopelessness and fear? I think the answer is that this type of encounter does something to our hearts. It flings our hearts open, allowing us to experience greater measures of God's love and presence than ever before. But this level of vulnerability to God's love can also leave us vulnerable to negative emotions, like anxiety and fear. That's why it is not uncommon to go from the thrill of victory into the throes of fear.

But this is not a negative thing! It is an invitation to let God in—not a problem to fix. In both victory and despair, we are forced to need God. And needing Him is the greatest gift God has given me in my life.

I love what happens next in the story of Elijah. In his moment of greatest weakness and despair, he experiences one of the most intimate encounters with God recorded in the Bible.

There is no formula for how and when God's provision will come.

At the end of his rope, and in his fatigue, Elijah falls asleep under a tree in the wilderness. When he wakes, he finds a divinely prepared meal of fresh bread and a jar of water. Elijah partakes of the meal and is strengthened.

God takes care of the weary prophet in the gentlest and most personal of ways. He leads him to His mountain and calls him to stand in His presence. Elijah's story culminates at the mouth of a cave, where God whispers to him in a still, small voice, assuring him of God's protection and provision.

Supporting One Another through Fear

At times our fears seem irrational, and we are embarrassed to talk about them. However, it is important that we share our fears with one another so that we can give each other the support and encouragement we all need. In doing so, we need to recognize that every fear is real in terms of how each individual experiences it. It is not helpful if we challenge someone's fears by saying, "You shouldn't be afraid of that." We ought to come alongside each other with compassionate concern, not minimizing another's fears with criticism or condemnation. We can recognize these fears, then speak the truth in love and pray together with faith.

My friend Jeff had an overwhelming fear of dogs. This fear began in his childhood; he could remember running in terror or being paralyzed in fear whenever a dog approached him. This fear was a source of embarrassment for Jeff, and it made him feel foolish. But years later, as a young adult, he humbled himself before someone and asked for prayer about this fear. When Jeff's friend prayed, something within Jeff broke. The next time he faced a dog, he was different—he could remain calm. Jeff would not say that the fear was completely gone, but it had lost its grip on him. It no longer controlled him as it had before. In Jeff's mind, it was clear that God had healed him. God had answered prayer and taken away something that had kept him in bondage.

I quit thinking about the possibility of dying
and fixed my eyes on the beauty of Jesus.

Sometimes when we invite Jesus into the midst of our fears and expect God's presence to lead us, we can completely break the power of fear. Other times, the person we pray for simply receives a quiet strength that enables him or her to walk forward in faith and courage. In each situation, we need to be sensitive to what God is doing and how that person is encountering God. We can do so much for each other, as we affirm both the reality of fear in our lives and the hope that we have in Jesus.

The Joy of Risky Obedience

There is no formula for how and when God's provision will come. God's watchful care over our lives does not always look the same. Sometimes God saves us from disaster, sometimes He gives us the strength to endure the storm, and sometimes we run away and He provides us with a safe place. God knows what we can handle, even if we do not. Our faith in Him pushes us to trust that He is involved in every aspect of our lives.

His presence amid my fear was worth more than having Him simply remove my fear from me.

When I first arrived in Afghanistan to begin working in the hospital, I was taken straight from the airport to the main office in Kabul for orientation. I was drinking tea in the corridor when someone approached me with a sheet of paper. It was a release form, which required my signature, stating that if I died in Afghanistan the organization would not be required to send my body home. At the time, I found it amusing. I was thinking, "Are you kidding me? I've been in this country for an hour, and this is what I have to do? Are they afraid I'll get shot before signing it? Welcome to Afghanistan!" I remember being flippant about it and even writing in the comment section, "Just throw my body in the local river."

Later that night, as I lay in bed, I began to wrestle with the implications of signing that form, and the reality of my situation hit me. The fear of death gripped my heart as I began to think I might die there. What if I never saw my family or friends again? The reality of living in a war zone became eerily palpable.

As I prayed, I surrendered my life into God's hands. Heaven filled my heart and I was overcome with joy. I could feel God's presence with me, and the fear of death began to lose its grip on me. I quit thinking about the possibility of dying and fixed my eyes on the beauty of Jesus.

Sometimes in our journey of faith, it happens like that. We encounter our fear, we run to Jesus with it, and we instantly see Him bring deliverance. Other times, it is quite different. I have another friend, Shelley, who spent several years serving God in Asia. She struggled for years with a significant fear of flying. Although it was painful for her to embrace this necessity of her calling and lifestyle, God proved Himself to her by helping her to endure the frequent flights. She made it through the times when her fear felt greater than her faith in God's protection. During the years she lived in Asia, she flew numerous times back to North America, to other parts of Asia, and to Europe. She came up against her fears each time she boarded a flight, but she would not let those fears stand in the way of the calling God had given her. She constantly focused on Jesus.

We do not need to be rid of our fears to be in love with Jesus and follow Him.

Is that what we consider victory over fear? Of course, Shelley would wish that her fears were completely gone, but they were not. She often told others about her fear and asked for prayer. She received support and encouragement, but the fears lingered. Although she still felt afraid, she continued to serve God and do what He was asking her to do. Her desire to follow God was greater than her fear of flying. Sometimes we experience victory only in part, or in stages.

I will never forget my first trip back to Afghanistan, eighteen months after my imprisonment in Iran. The Taliban was running the country, and the only way to get into Kabul, the capital, was by bus from Pakistan. In the final days of preparation, I realized I was filled with fear. Just a year earlier, I had attempted to return to Afghanistan but succumbed to fear and ended up canceling my trip. I knew God had called me, but I was afraid. This time, I decided to rebuke the fear and stand against it. But it did not leave completely.

Why does Jesus let us get into trouble?

Just before getting on the bus, I stopped and prayed, looking to Jesus and letting His beauty overwhelm me. I was still afraid, but I wanted to please Him more than I wanted to be rid of my fears, so I got on the bus. Throughout the fifteen-hour journey, I experienced Jesus's love and protection in such a way that they became more real than the fears I was facing. His presence amid my fear was worth more than having Him simply remove my fears from me.

I meet people around the world who have great concern for their safety. A number of them hold back from living in risky obedience because those fears have not yet been relieved. However, we do not need to be rid of our fears to be in love with Jesus and follow Him. The more I am overwhelmed by Jesus and put my focus on Him, the more I find the power to obey Him and do what He asks—whether or not my fears ever leave. Getting over my fears should not be my preoccupation. My focus should be discovering Jesus.

One of my favorite Bible stories, Matthew 14:22–33, says a great deal about how we are to address safety issues within our life of faith. Jesus speaks to the crowds and then goes up the mountain by Himself to pray. Meanwhile, He sends His disciples across the lake in a boat, but they get caught in a storm. Jesus decides to go out and meet them, walking out on the water in middle of the roiling lake. As soon as the disciples see Jesus on the water, they are terrified, thinking He is a ghost. Instead of calming the storm, Jesus speaks to them. "Take courage! It is I. Do not be afraid" (v. 27).

Why does He do that? Why does Jesus let us get into trouble? Why does He allow storms into our lives? Imagine His disciples—out on the lake, trapped in the raging waters, without Him. They were frightened by the storm, but Jesus came to them with words of comfort and peace. I think it is significant that Jesus met them in the midst of the storm but let them struggle for a while. He allowed them to experience their weakness and fear before saving them.

It is the nature of love to push us beyond what is normal and into new realms of possibility.

Peter's response was particularly special. He was a risk taker, often getting into trouble with his quick words and deeds, and here he saw the opportunity for something amazing. He called out to Jesus, "Lord, if it's you . . . tell me to come to you on the water," and Jesus told him, "Come" (vv. 28–29). Peter walked out on the water! He joined Jesus and defied natural law. At first, I think Peter was probably as scared as the rest of the disciples, but after he heard the voice of Jesus, he somehow got the idea that he could do what Jesus was doing. He was beginning to realize that he could obey Jesus, even when he felt afraid, even when what Jesus was doing was impossible.

Peter's love for Jesus pushed him to obey, no matter the cost. Peter was willing to step out of the boat and into the wild waves, just because Jesus was already there. It is the nature of love to push us beyond what is normal and into new realms of possibility. As we walk in faith, it becomes part of our natural process to wonder what could happen if we responded to Jesus even more deeply and embraced the life He has modeled for us. Stepping out in faith is always a risk. The new ground is unfamiliar and often chaotic, and we waver from time to time. The key is that Jesus is there. His presence makes all the difference. His hand is never far from ours, and He invites us, saying, "Come."

What happened to Peter? After experiencing a few miraculous steps on top of the waves, he took his eyes off Jesus and began to sink. The story says that Jesus immediately reached out His hand and caught him. I wonder what was going through Peter's mind. I wonder if he regretted stepping out of the boat. I can only imagine the smile on Peter's face as he embraced Jesus and they got back into the boat together. I would guess that he never regretted those few miraculous steps and never forgot how amazing a life trusting Jesus could be.

I have often heard undue emphasis placed on the fact that Peter took his eyes off Jesus and almost drowned. I do not believe that is the message God wants us to take from this story. Jesus is bigger than our failures as we step out in faith. Peter was able to share one of the most miraculous moments in the Bible, with Jesus Himself. Peter discovered safety in the midst of fear as he focused on Jesus. We are all on this journey of learning to trust Jesus more and more. He invites each one of us to embrace a lifestyle of risk-taking obedience, wherever we are. He does not want us to worry about our safety; He does not want fear to hold us back. He wants us to base our decisions, not on what seems safe, but on something more than our own fear—the promise that He will watch over us and protect us.

There is no government, no health code, no insurance company, no rule, and no place that can guarantee our safety. Jesus invites each one of us to take steps of faith, to explore how amazing life can be with Him, to trust Him in the middle of our fears. He is not asking us to do anything that He has not done, or go anywhere He has not been. He simply calls us to move beyond our fears and respond to all that He asks us to do. Jesus invites us to walk with Him into the most amazing life we could possibly know.

Jesus, thank You for protecting me. Help me not to get stuck worrying about my safety, but to simply trust in You and embrace a lifestyle of risk-taking obedience. I know that You will watch over me and protect me and that You will be with me wherever I go. Help me step out of the boat. Help me to move beyond my fears and to live the life that You are calling me to live, to gaze on Your beauty and let it overwhelm my fears. Amen.

chapter six

Fear and Identity

O ur identities are connected to our sense of worth. When our sense of worth becomes skewed, we become prone to the fear of man, the fear of rejection, and the fear of being alone.

There is no fear more prevalent than the fear of what other people think of us. Almost everything we do, from how we dress, to the way we talk, to even the profession we choose, can be influenced by fear of what others will think or say. This fear is an invisible prison. For some of us, the fear of man—when we are more concerned about what others think about us or the decisions we are about to make than in what God thinks—is more of an issue in our youth, but it affects many of us throughout our lives.

What if we could live free from what others think about us—free from worrying about everyone else's opinion? This has been one of the major dreams of my life. The beautiful reality is, I have found a place of freedom in my identity through understanding God's heart for me.

Allowing Jesus to Shape Our Identity

I grew up as a Christian, but for many years I never really understood the unconditional love of God. In fact, I had always struggled with the phrase "unconditional love." How could God love or even like me? I didn't even like me. I believed God's love was unconditional but thought, "He would probably love me more if I hadn't done this." I subconsciously wondered what I could do to make Him love me more. To me, being a Christian was about doing the right thing and not doing the wrong thing. It was not about a relationship or friendship with the living God.

What if we could live free from what others think about us?

All of this changed when I was sixteen. I was at a retreat in the mountains of California where Steve Fry, who currently pastors in Nashville, Tennessee, was speaking.

"Everything you do for God needs to come from the overflow of intimacy with God," he said.

He repeated this statement over and over. That afternoon, I found myself standing on the bank of a river, thinking about what he had said. I wanted to do things for God. But if everything I did for God had to come from intimacy with God, I needed to figure out what "intimacy with God" was. As I struggled to solve this problem, I picked up some rocks and began to throw them into the water. Suddenly, I heard a voice in my head.

"Hey, Dan, can I throw rocks with you?"

What is that? I thought. The voice came again.

"Hey, Dan, can I throw rocks with you?"

For the next few minutes, I heard the question over and over again. I knew it wasn't my own voice, and it certainly wasn't the devil's. Could that be God?! No way. God has a lot of things on His mind. Why would He care about me throwing rocks? But even as I attempted to rationalize it away, the question persisted. Finally, I stopped and looked up to God.

"Yes!" I said. "If this is You, yes, You can throw rocks with me. But why?"

Immediately, I felt God reply.

"Because you want to throw rocks."

"That's it?"

"Yeah, that's it."

I was blown away. That was what intimacy with God meant! He liked me! If I wanted to go for a walk, He wanted to go for a walk. If I wanted to go to the beach, He wanted to go to the beach—not just to make sure I was doing something spiritual, but simply because He enjoyed my company. From then on, everything changed. For the first time, I began to believe that an intimate relationship with God wasn't just for pastors or those who were "really spiritual"—it was for me. I had discovered that God loved me unconditionally. There was nothing I could ever do to make Him love me more and nothing I could do to make Him love me less.

"This is my Son, whom I love; with him I am well pleased" (Matt. 3:17). God said this before Jesus was involved in any public ministry, before He healed anyone, before He performed any of the miracles for which He became known. Isn't it amazing that God's clear affirmation of love comes before all that? God's love for His Son had nothing to do with what His Son would accomplish. It was complete before His Son did anything. God's love for us is the same! Do we hear the words of the Father speaking into our hearts and saying, "You are My child, whom I love; in you I am well pleased"? Perhaps

we need to slow down, quiet our hearts before God, and listen
for those words. Nothing will change our lives more than the
gentle words of love and affirmation we hear from our heavenly Father.

---

*Take time with God to work through identity
issues, filtering through the noise in life that so
easily distracts us from asking the hard questions.*

From that day on, I found myself in a sweet and innocent
relationship with my Father in heaven. I was learning to find
my identity in simply being His beloved child. There was
nothing more secure in my world than God's love for me, and
it seemed only natural to respond by opening my heart and
loving Him back.

After college, as I continued to live from this place of freedom and discovery, God dropped Afghanistan into my heart.
As the idea grew stronger within me, I realized I was content
to spend the rest of my life serving God in a remote village—
God's love was motivating me. I didn't need recognition from
others; I didn't need a prominent position or an impressive salary. I didn't care if anyone knew my name. I was so completely
satisfied in my relationship with Jesus that I was ready to live
and die in relative obscurity just to have the opportunity to
share His love with people who didn't know Him. So I went.

During my latter years working in Afghanistan, I began
to realize that my identity had become skewed. The innocence
I had known and enjoyed in my friendship with Jesus had,
somehow, become tainted. There was a growing acknowledg-
ment among friends and acquaintances of how awesome I was
for working in Afghanistan, for living there during the war,

and for serving the poor. I was grateful and encouraged by how my life was positively affecting others. But over time, the accolades I was receiving from people were becoming more important than what God said about me. My identity was no longer rooted in the simple beauty of being a child of God.

A few years later, after I left Afghanistan, I took the fateful trip to Iran that led to my imprisonment. After my miraculous release, I abruptly found myself back in America, where suddenly my prison story made me a hero. This only intensified my struggle with identity. People welcomed me, saying, "Wow, you're such a man of God. I could never do that," or "You're so strong. You remind me of Paul." Once again, I began to define myself by my accomplishments and what others thought about me.

The fear of man causes us to measure our worth by things outside our core identity in God.

As I considered what I should do next, I immediately felt led to stay back and serve at a small YWAM base in southern Colorado. At the same time, people were asking, "So what's next, Dan? What's the next great thing you're going to do for God?" I felt as though everyone's expectations of me were rising, and I began to resent the call to stay in Colorado. I wanted to move back overseas and do something "radical" for God so people would continue to praise me.

Something was not right in my heart. Why did I care so much about what people were thinking? Why, all of a sudden, did I have to do the next "great thing"? Why was I no longer okay with being out in the middle of nowhere, following Jesus and not seeking any other approval, like I used to be?

As I began to unravel when and why the source of my identity changed, I realized it was not just a result of people's praises of my service in Afghanistan or their comments about my imprisonment. The seed of my struggles with identity began in my younger years.

As I was growing up, certain comments people made and ideas they had insinuated deeply affected me. No one person said these words to me, but this is what my heart heard: "Dan, if you really want to serve God, you should get involved in the church. You should teach Sunday school or help with the summer camp. If you're really serious about God, you should go on a short-term mission trip. And if you're really committed, you should sign up for a discipleship program and get some longer-term missions experience. If you're really radical, you'll actually become a missionary and live overseas. If you're really, really radical, you'll end up in the Muslim world. But the most radical thing you could do for God, the ultimate act of service and surrender, would be to get imprisoned and martyred for your faith."

To put it in modern terms, God's crazy about us!

As I pondered these things, I realized I was in the throes of an identity crisis. The opinions of others were now guiding my decisions and driving my identity. The simple sincerity of being in love with Jesus, and letting everything flow from that, was becoming obscured by what other people thought of me. I still wanted to do what Jesus told me, but only as it resonated with approval from everyone around me—especially those who saw me as some kind of Christian superhero.

I will never forget what happened next. It was a Sunday

evening, and my dear friend and mentor Sally McClung came to pray for me. In brokenness, I opened my heart and told her everything I was going through. Sally looked me straight in the eye.

"Dan," she said, "the greatest accomplishment you will ever achieve in this life is to be known as a child of God."

It was simple but profound, and at that moment something within me broke. I knew that Sally's words came straight from God's heart. Tears began to roll down my face as I absorbed this truth about my identity. I began to realize how I had gone astray by focusing on what others thought of me and not on what Jesus thought of me. I cried out to Jesus and asked Him to change my heart.

That evening was a turning point for me. My identity was in the process of being restored back to simplicity. In the days and weeks to come, I became more and more focused on God's love for me and what He had done for me. I found myself resting more in God and enjoying my identity as His child. Suddenly, the big question of what I should do next with my life became very simple: Wake up, ask Jesus what to do, and do it. I decided to say yes to God's prompting to serve at the YWAM base in southern Colorado. Although it might have looked like taking a step back from being a "radical" overseas Christian worker, I was filled with peace because I knew it was the next thing Jesus wanted me to do. For three years, I stayed in Colorado, loving the simple life God had given me.

Jesus found all of His identity in being the Son of God, no matter what it looked like day to day. Some days He got the praise of the masses, and some days we know nothing about and have no idea if anyone noticed what He did! Jesus was always content, because His identity was found in His Father's love for Him. He invites us to live the same way. It is so important for us to take time with God to work through our identity issues, filtering through the noise in our lives that so easily distracts us from asking the hard questions. We need to run back to Jesus again and again, asking Him to speak to us and clarify who we are in His eyes. We need to find ways to regularly refocus our hearts on what is essential. I have a close friend who prays the same simple prayer every day: "Lord Jesus, I belong to you. Nothing matters more than that."

Having an identity rooted in God's love is the only way to freedom from the fear of man. While attending a conference in Colorado, I was privileged to spend a few days with my close friend Darlene Cunningham. Darlene is the cofounder of YWAM and a leader I greatly admire. Darlene invited me to lead an upcoming training school at YWAM's University of the Nations in Kona, Hawaii. I was honored that she would ask me and immediately told her I would pray about it.

If you had one free afternoon, would you rather spend it with a highly acclaimed leader or a homeless guy downtown?

Later that day, I considered the opportunity. I was again struck by what a privilege it was to be given this chance by Darlene. I did not feel specific direction from the Lord as I prayed. All I felt was that I should say yes, because it was Darlene who was asking me. I went to Darlene and said I would do it.

During the next three weeks, as I began to prepare for the school, I became increasingly aware that I did not feel peace about leading it. Nothing was coming together as I had hoped, and I couldn't find anyone who was willing to help me. The more I thought about the school, the more uneasy I felt.

Eventually, I expressed some of my inner turmoil to Darlene and asked her to pray for me about whether or not I had made the right decision.

Finally, five weeks before the school was to start, Darlene called and told me she needed a final answer from me about leading the school. As I paused and prayed, I began to quiver with fear. I felt completely stuck. I wanted to do what was right, and I knew I didn't have a peace in my heart to go ahead, but I trembled at the thought of letting Darlene down. With tears running down my face, I apologized to Darlene and told her no. My hand shook the entire time. I felt terrible knowing how disappointed she would be.

Our phone call ended abruptly. "Okay," Darlene said and hung up the phone.

My heart felt sick. I went to my room and began to pray. I knew I had initially made my decision based on the fear of man. I had not prayed about it; I only wanted to please Darlene. I was sincere in my desire to serve, but I was less focused on what God wanted me to do and more concerned about what one of my leaders wanted me to do.

I decided to ask the Lord for forgiveness. As I did, something happened to me that had never happened before in my life. As soon as I said the words "I'm sorry," a dark cloud came out of my mouth and floated toward the open window. I sat there completely frozen and freaked out! What was that?

Then I realized it—the dark cloud was an attack of the enemy on my life. Satan was doing everything he could to keep me from doing what God wanted. By giving in to the fear of man, I had opened the door for this attack. The moment I humbled myself before God, the attack of the enemy visibly left, in the form of that black cloud.

I sat there and trembled at the severity of the moment. Then peace and joy began flooding my heart. I had made the right decision to obey God and not lead the school. Doing what God wanted was more important than what my leaders thought. I gave thanks to God and walked boldly into the next six months of my life, knowing that He wanted to bless me and lead me. It turned out to be the most fruitful six months in my life thus far. I also was able to meet with Darlene, and our friendship continues to grow and be blessed.

The fear of man causes us to measure our worth by things outside our core identity in God. Ultimately, we must get our sense of significance from our Creator. He loves us completely, and we are always under His watchful eye, no matter what we do or what our title is, and no matter what people say about us. To put it in modern terms, God's crazy about us!

What's more, Jesus finds equal worth in all people, no matter what title or status others give them. Do you think more highly of "Tom the prophet" than you do of "Bill the plumber"? Do you think God does? If you had one free afternoon, would you rather spend it with a highly acclaimed leader or a homeless guy downtown? Frank the apostle, John the evangelist, Mark the accountant, Joanne the premed student, Dan the garbage collector, and Jean the homeless drunk—all these people are created in the image of God. As we study the life of Jesus, we see His organic flow of love and engagement with whoever came into His life. People of high status, people of low status, even people who were about to be stoned—Jesus loved and valued them all. He freely gave of His time and energy to invest in each person His Father led Him to.

There is no one I have seen model this better than Loren Cunningham when I had the privilege of traveling with him for many months. Loren's schedule allowed him to meet key leaders in the body of Christ as well as heads of state, yet I often saw him leave a conversation with a highly recognized leader to spend time with eighteen- and nineteen-year-olds. He was equally excited to be engaged in their lives. Status didn't matter to Loren, because he follows Jesus's example in seeing every person's equal value.

It's natural for people to have different titles and roles in society. You may be a teacher, a mother, a lawyer, or an architect, but these roles were never meant to define your self-worth. Titles and roles do not determine what Jesus thinks of us, and they shouldn't determine how we think of ourselves or others.

Every life lived in surrender to God is ministry.

Is being a pastor better than having a "normal job"? To be honest, I have sometimes considered certain jobs more valuable than others. We often see only those who work full-time in roles like pastor or evangelist as "being in the ministry" and thus see those jobs as somehow "better." But shouldn't each of us just do what we feel God is telling us to do? If God tells me to go work at McDonald's, would He rather I serve Him overseas? If I love God with all that I am, I will respond in obedience to whatever God prompts me to do. This conviction also frees me from judging other people and their vocations because I simply believe that, as they find their identity in God, their choice of vocation is a response to His love.

Sometimes people ask me, "Dan, should we all get involved in the ministry?" I usually respond by saying, "Yes, we are all involved in the ministry." Ministry is simply the outworking of our obedience. It's what happens when we offer ourselves to God and use our gifts to serve others. Every life lived in surrender to God is ministry. If we are faithful in obedience, simply doing the next thing Jesus has asked of us, we are fulfilling the ministry to which He has called us.

What if we caught the vision for being ourselves wherever God has placed us and whatever He has called us to do? Whether as a carpenter or a student, we can find the secret of being content and having joy in simple devotion to God. We can embrace Paul's exhortation, "Work willingly at whatever you do, as though you were working for the Lord rather than for people" (Col. 3:23 NLT).

Fear of Loneliness

When I first began to consider working in Afghanistan, I was twenty-two years old and single. I was very excited about the opportunity to serve overseas, but I was also struggling with the fear of being alone. When I finally agreed to go, there were still six months before the assignment began. I honestly thought that during those six months I would get married. But the six months passed, and I was still single.

In my head I knew I wasn't alone and He was with me, but it just didn't feel like it.

Have you ever told God, "God, I know You are enough, but I want to get married," or "God, I know that You completely satisfy my heart, but I still want to get married"? That was exactly what was going on inside of me. I wanted to get married in order to satisfy a level of discontent in my heart. What I needed was a greater revelation of God. Could it be that there was enough of Him to actually satisfy me completely, in every way?

I knew that my chances of finding a spouse in Afghanistan were slim. I also knew that nothing was impossible with God and that Adam was asleep when God provided Eve, so I could be anywhere, doing anything when God provided a spouse for me! But I began to sense God saying that He wanted to be enough for me; He wanted to be my satisfaction. I felt that God was speaking into my heart and calling me to love and trust Him more.

I will never forget the day I flew into Afghanistan for the first time. I flew from Delhi, India, to Kabul, Afghanistan, on a Boeing 737. As I settled down in my seat, 16D, I looked around and realized I was the only white person on the plane. There were over 150 Afghans and me!

About fifteen minutes into the flight I was hit by a rush of emotion, and I cried out to God. "Why are You sending me to Afghanistan all alone?"

I heard God respond gently to my heart. "You're not alone."

Not ten minutes later, the emotions rushed through my body again. I felt extremely alone. Again, I cried out to God, and again, He responded, "You're not alone." Twenty minutes later, it happened again—why was it so hard to believe God about this? In my head I knew I wasn't alone and He was with me, but it just didn't feel like it. I cried out a third time, and this time, God whispered something to my heart.

"Dan, do you know what is happening right now at the airport in Kabul, Afghanistan?"

"No."

"Do you want to see?"

"Yes, please!"

Sitting in my seat, about forty-five minutes from arriving in Kabul, I saw this vision:

Jesus and another man are standing at the airport, near a

fence overlooking the tarmac. They are waiting for incoming flights.

"Why are you here?" Jesus asks the other man.

"I have a business contact coming in today," the man replies. "Why are You here?"

"Dan is coming!" Jesus says, brimming with excitement.

"Who is Dan?"

"Who is Dan? You don't know? Dan is My friend, My really good friend, and he is coming here to see Me! I can't wait to see him!"

They continue to wait. Suddenly, there is noise from an incoming aircraft. As it lands, Jesus runs to the fence.

"I wonder if that's Dan's plane!" He yells above the noise.

As the plane taxis to a halt in front of the fence, Jesus sees that it's not my plane and walks back to the man. They continue waiting. Jesus begins to rock back and forth on His feet, a huge smile on His face.

The man looks at Jesus, confused. "What's Your problem?"

"I'm just so excited that Dan's coming!"

"Why are You so excited?"

"You have no idea! Dan is a really close friend of mine, and he thinks I invited him here just to serve the Afghan people. But the main reason I invited him here is so our friendship can grow. And this is the best place to do that!"

There is the noise of another plane, and again, Jesus runs to the fence, waiting for it to taxi in. When He sees it is my plane, He turns around with a huge smile on His face.

"Dan must be on this one!"

When the plane comes to a stop, the staircase is pushed to the door, and people begin to exit. As I walk out of the plane, Jesus sees me from the fence. He looks at the man He is with, joy emanating from His face.

"There he is! Dan has come to be with Me!"

The vision ended. Tears were rolling down my face.

"Is this true?" I asked God.

"Yes, it is."

I felt God looking down on me with a big smile.

"Jesus, are You saying the main reason You invited me to Afghanistan was just to be with You? Just so our friendship would get closer?"

"Yes, Dan. That's exactly why I asked you to come!"

I was overwhelmed by the revelation of God's friendship and love for me. I truly was not alone! It was that simple. My fears had been overcome by the love of Jesus. I knew I could endure whatever challenges living in Afghanistan would bring, because Jesus was with me.

Over the next ten years, I often looked back on that experience, and it gave me strength to press on. I still wonder if I will get married, but for now Jesus has given me great joy in being single and having friendship with Him. Ultimately, the fear of loneliness has been yet another invitation to come closer to God and discover I am His son.

Today I find myself tagged as an author, a missionary, a teacher, a public speaker, a single man, and an ex-convict. Although these titles are given to me from time to time in various contexts, I am increasingly aware of my own need to be content with being a child of God. What I do brings me recognition, and it is so easy to slip back into measuring my worth based on that recognition. A few years ago, my good friend Amy Sollars saw me struggling with this and challenged me to walk away from my identity as "the guy who was imprisoned in Iran." I took her advice and pursued being known solely as a child of God, loved by the Father. It is that simple. His love is enough.

Sometimes it's good to stop and be reminded that you are just a child of God. More than anything else, it is God's love for you that defines who you are. There is nothing more foundational to our identity. As we realize we are loved unconditionally, the fear of man, fear of rejection, and fear of being alone all become less consuming. We are free to simply be lovers of God.

Jesus, thank You for making me just the way I am. Help me to find my identity in You. Thank You for Your love that embraces me and calls me Your own. I want to find that place of security and safety in Your arms. Help me to be more concerned about what You think of me than what others think of me. Help me to be content with Your companionship and at peace with my identity as Your child. As I find my identity in You, help me to live a life of simply responding to Your love by loving You back. Amen.

chapter seven

Embracing Our Weakness

*J*ust before starting this book, I had the privilege of
speaking to more than a hundred high school students
at a summer discipleship seminar. As I sat in the front row,
preparing to get up and teach, everything inside me was confronted by the thought that I am not particularly relevant. I
felt weak, insignificant. I sat there trying to think of what I
could say to relate to a bunch of teenagers. I was afraid my stories were too old and too unimportant to influence their lives.
As I sat and prayed, Jesus clearly challenged me to share my
heart, to be myself, and to step out in my weakness. I am so
glad He did, because many of the students gave testimonies of
how my stories radically challenged them and impacted their
hearts.

We do not like to be seen as vulnerable. We do not like
our weaknesses to be exposed; it frightens us. It is often the
case that our fear is motivated by a dislike for feeling weak.
Of course we would rather feel confident. But fear is an open
invitation to run to God—and so is our weakness. For most

of us, feeling weak triggers a reactionary impulse to get rid of our weakness, or somehow hide it. I would like to propose that weakness is actually a good thing. In fact, weakness is a gift! Anything that causes us to run to God in this life is a gift.

God invites all of us, confident or not, to live a life of total dependence on Jesus.

Weakness has been as central to my journey with Jesus as fear. For much of my early life, I suffered from a cripplingly low self-esteem. I was quiet, timid, and devoid of self-confidence. I spent most of my teen years sitting alone in my room; I felt awkward and just wanted to avoid people. I never felt the power to make even simple decisions in life—I felt too weak. I avoided anyone who was loud or came across as strong. When others shared their opinions, I kept quiet, not because I didn't have something to say, but because I felt unable to initiate and speak out. I felt trapped inside myself.

Self-confidence seems to be one of the attributes prized in our society. It's pushed by our media, our education system, and our free-market economy. If you want to be successful, it seems, you need to be very sure of yourself. This idea is also pushed in Christian circles. Confidence is not a bad thing to have and, to be honest, I would like to feel it more often myself. However, I am very aware that confidence in myself is not what I need in order to have a successful life of joy, peace, and obedience with God.

I have struggled to feel confident in doing things my entire life. The good news is, there is something much greater than feeling self-confident. When we walk with Jesus, He gives us the strength and power to do everything He has called us to do. I have been tempted not to move forward in obedience until I felt confident in myself. However, as I look back on my life, my joy has always been in my relationship with God and obedience to Him, not in a sense of self-assurance. I have joy in my constant, unchanging relationship with God, whether I feel confident or not. If you naturally have a bold sense of confidence, I admire that. But God invites all of us, confident or not, to live a life of total dependence on Jesus. From that dependence, we can step out in faith to do the next thing He tells us to do.

Jesus invites us to be confident in what He has said and who He is. We may not always feel confident in ourselves, in our circumstances, or in our ability to accomplish what He has asked of us. Regardless, we can always be sure that He is with us.

We are terrified that if our true selves, with their flaws and frailties, are revealed, people will look down on us or, worse, reject us.

When I went to Iran, I was confident God had told me to go. I felt God clearly calling me to Iran for two weeks. But the process of actually going exposed a lot of weakness in me. At first I was certain He had told me to go, but in the ensuing three months my weakness began to surface and shake my confidence. Some days I wondered if I would be turned away at the border, or imprisoned there. Other days I was afraid my leaders would disapprove of my decision to go. I began to doubt that I had heard God correctly. Even so, I decided to focus on God in the midst of my weakness and obey what I felt He had told me to do. As I look back at that time, I am so glad I went to Iran. Although I felt weak, I pressed in to God, walking forward in dependence every step of the way. Today, my Iran experience is a testimony to God's goodness and has allowed me to minister powerfully to many, many people.

Dependence upon Jesus is vital to our walk with God. Many of us, however, see dependence as a natural attribute only in children. It is true that as we develop from children into adults, we become less and less dependent upon our parents. But God calls us not only to depend upon Jesus but to grow in dependence on Him throughout our lives.

I was sure God was telling me to do something, but I felt completely weak and incapable of doing it.

Jesus tells us that if we want to enter the kingdom of heaven, we must become like children. There are different aspects of childlikeness. Some are good and need to stay with us for the rest of our lives; these include growing in the Lord, learning, and maintaining total dependence on God. There are other aspects we need to walk away from as we mature. Being like children in this sense is often referred to as being "childish" and includes immaturity, obstinacy, and rashness. The kind of childlikeness Jesus calls us to is the kind He models for us when He says, "The Son . . . does only what he sees the Father doing" (John 5:19 NLT). Jesus also talks about how He and the Father are one (John 17). Jesus lived in total dependence on His Father throughout His whole life, and He invites us to do the same.

Why is dependency such a struggle for us? I believe it is because we are afraid to be weak. We would much rather be known by our strengths than our weaknesses. We are terrified that if our true selves, with their flaws and frailties, are revealed, people will look down on us or, worse, reject us. Sometimes these fears are based on painful experiences of ridicule or rejection by a friend, a leader, a parent, or a spouse. In response, we vowed never to make ourselves vulnerable again. We have been hiding, and avoiding self-exposure at all costs, ever since. Maybe, in order to mask our pain and weakness, we act strong on the outside, but on the inside we are anxious and afraid. To some extent, we all do this—we are all hiding vulnerabilities from each other.

On the other side of the fears that keep us hiding, there is a deep longing within us to be known for who we really are. It is the cry of every human heart to be known. We yearn to be our real selves with people, with ourselves, and with God. This is our God-given desire for intimacy, unconditional love, and acceptance. God's heart for each one of us is to set us free so we can be who He has created us to be. As we surrender to God's love, He empowers us to be honest and open about our weaknesses—to be known by others for who we really are.

Our confidence should not be rooted in our ability to hear God. It should be rooted in His goodness toward us.

As we become sure of what God thinks of us, we have increased freedom to step out in obedience even when we feel weak. In the fall of 2002, I felt that God was speaking to me about writing a second book. My first book, Imprisoned in Iran, had been a great success. Despite that, as I began to think about writing another book, my heart was in turmoil. I was confronted by my fears and insecurities. I was sure God was telling me to do something, but I felt completely weak and incapable of doing it. In some ways, it would have been easy for me to give up on the idea of another book. However, God did not let me. He kept bringing it to mind, and I kept leaning on Him and committing it to prayer, even though I still had my doubts. My first book had simply been my story, but I felt that this second book was meant to explore the theological foundations of my faith journey. I am no scholar, and I questioned whether I really had anything significant to say and whether I could ever complete the task on my own.

God is more interested in, committed to, and capable of helping us find His will for our lives than we could ever be.

After some time, I was led to contact my friend Mark Klassen and to ask him about helping me write the book. I will never forget when Mark and I met to discuss the project; in the midst of my fear and weakness, God gave me the power to choose faith and obedience. We worked on the project for eight days. Mark and I had a strong resolve that there was enough material for a new book.

Just when we were ready to move forward, Mark's hard drive crashed, and it appeared that all our work had been lost. We were heartbroken, but with desperate faith we laid our hands on the computer and prayed, "God, we know this is Your project, and we ask that You resurrect all the work we've done." Miraculously, the computer rebooted and we had just enough time to save the material to another disk. We had a mere ten minutes before the computer crashed and died permanently.

In early 2005, A Beautiful Way was published, and it became an important teaching tool for me for years to come. As I look back, I am amazed at what God did through me, despite my insecurity and fear. Remarkably, that book has encouraged tens of thousands of people in their journeys with Jesus. Our own stories of obedience often greatly encourage others. So, too, do the stories of others encourage us.

As for me, I love the stories of how the disciple Peter models risk-taking obedience. Although he failed many times, his failures never defined or eliminated the fruit that God would bring from his life. Peter is heralded as a great man of faith, and we are amazed by his transformation in the book of Acts. Just months before, Peter had allowed fear to coerce him into denying Jesus. In Acts 2, he is a different man. When the Holy Spirit falls in the upper room, thousands gather to see what is going on. Peter addresses the amassed crowd; in faith, he stands up and proclaims the goodness of God, and thousands are added to the kingdom.

I stopped asking "why" and just believed that God would always be looking out for my good.

Peter was a disciple. To be a disciple means to be a learner. No one expects a learner to be perfect in knowledge or experience. They are supposed to be free to make mistakes. We need to follow this example. We need to let it be okay to fail and make mistakes as we walk with Jesus. Scripture says that, though He was perfect, Jesus Himself grew and learned. "Jesus grew in wisdom and stature, and in favor with God and men" (Luke 2:52), and He learned obedience from what He suffered (Heb. 5:8). Through it all, Jesus embraced weakness.

He was the uncreated God, but chose to be born as a helpless infant and grow up completely dependent upon his parents to care for Him. If you are growing and learning, you are being like Jesus, and that is a good thing!

Another area of weakness I have struggled with in my own life is the inability to hear God perfectly. If I had perfect guidance, I could step out in total confidence when making decisions. But sometimes I hesitate to make decisions because I am not sure that I heard right. And sometimes I feel 100 percent sure I heard God—but it turns out I was wrong. We all hate making mistakes; we want to be strong, wise, and certain, especially when it comes to our relationship with God. But our confidence should not be rooted in our ability to hear Him. It should be rooted in His goodness toward us.

God shares our pain. He knows our struggle. He is present with us when we endure suffering.

It is more important for us to have confidence in God's character than to have the ability to be completely accurate. God is more interested in, committed to, and capable of helping us find His will for our lives than we could ever be.

We need to run to Him with everything. But as we run to Him with everything, often what He wants is not clear. If we have gotten it wrong in the past, and we feel unsure of what God wants, it is very easy to give up on including God in our decisions and instead base our decisions solely on what feels right or logical. God never meant for us to be upset when we don't know exactly what to do. The joy of running to Him and getting to know Him is better than the joy of being 100 percent sure.

I have often tried to be absolutely sure I am hearing from God before I ever make a decision. But this approach is stifling. Many times I'm not totally sure what I'm hearing is right. But that is okay! It is far better to embrace the weakness of our attempts to hear God and take the risk of doing what we sense He is saying. That is how we discover who He is, which is ultimately what He wants.

In most of the decisions I make, I feel 51–99 percent sure I'm hearing from God.* This means I have more of a sense that something is the right thing to do; I have more peace than less peace. Realizing this has helped me make decisions without becoming paralyzed by anxiety and fear when I am not totally sure. What I am sure of is who He is: He is good, He is for me, and He will guide me.

It is critical to remember this. Because sometimes we will get it wrong. During the years I worked in Afghanistan, I made a visit to my parents' home in southern California, where I had spent my childhood. One day during the visit, I heard these simple words in my heart.

"Your dad will die when he is eighty-five."

At the time my father was fifty-five, and I did not know what to think. Could this really be the voice of God? Why would He tell me something like this? I told no one about what I heard, but over the years I began to cherish it and grow in confidence that God had indeed spoken to me. I loved my dad, and as hard as it was to imagine that someday he would pass away, there was sweet comfort in knowing that he would be with us into his old age.

During the next fifteen years, the word about his death at the age of eighty-five came to me again and again, giving me assurance and hope. If you had asked me eight years ago if I

---

* See chapter 9.

had ever been really, really sure about hearing God in my life, I would have said yes, and I would have pointed to this word concerning my dad's death. God gave me so many confirmations of this word. I remember one year when God spoke it to me again, and I replied, "God, if this is really You, I pray the next car that passes me is green." I turned around and there was a green car. Similar specific and dramatic experiences confirmed this message to my heart over and over again. I was sure God had spoken to me. It was the most certain I had ever felt about hearing a word from God.

In November 2006 my father was diagnosed with leukemia, and three months later he died. He was seventy-nine years old. In the midst of my grief, I found myself in a dilemma: the thing I was most confident in hearing God's voice about had turned out to be wrong. If I had heard God wrong about this, what about everything else? How could I ever be certain about hearing from God again? As I thought about this, I became incredibly sad and disappointed. For weeks, I poured out my heart to God, asking for clarity on why I had heard Him wrong all these years, and I heard nothing in response. Do you ever hear silence when you talk to God? Weeks went by, until I finally realized I might never understand. In my heart, I wanted to give up on the idea of hearing from God. The more I analyzed the situation, the sadder I became.

About two months after my dad passed away, I woke up in the morning and confronted God.

"I'm done," I said. "I'm done trying to figure out what went wrong. I'm done trying to understand why this word about my dad's death wasn't true. I give up!"

I poured out my heart to God and let it go. I chose to believe that God was good, no matter what had happened with my dad. I decided to move forward, to believe that God would still speak to me. I stopped asking why and just believed that

God would always be looking out for my good. Everything changed when I chose to trust Him. As soon as I prayed that prayer, I entered into a deep peace that lingered throughout the day and into the night.

When I awoke the next morning, I heard the voice of God again for the first time in months. It was a gentle whisper in my heart.

"Thank you, my son, for trusting Me. I love you and have wonderful things in store for you."

At that moment, joy returned to my heart and I had a renewed sense of purpose. From then on, I began to expect to hear His voice as I had before.

If we have God's call to do something
but feel weak, let us run to Jesus, lean
on Him, and walk forward.

It is humbling to bring our questions and frustrations to God. It requires us to admit that we do not know, that we cannot be sure, and that we need help. We all experience things in life that are difficult, sometimes impossible, to understand. We get confused, and we wonder why things work out the way they do. We feel we need to understand the reasons behind what happens in our lives, and when we do not, we doubt God's goodness. I know I tend to overanalyze situations and expect answers I can make sense of.

We can hold onto unmet expectations and become angry and bitter; we can stay in the place of hurt and wallow in disappointment. Each of these responses steals our joy and causes us to feel distance between God and ourselves. When my father died and I saw that my expectations concerning what God had said were wrong, I found myself asking, "Is God still good?"

I was asking the wrong questions. In the end, the question was not "Why did I hear God wrong?" or "Why did Dad die at age seventy-nine instead of eighty-five?" It was "How will I move forward?" I remember that morning so clearly. I told God, "From this day forward, I make the choice to trust Your character above this experience. I choose to never ask You the why question regarding my dad's death ever again. I choose to believe that You are good, I choose to believe that You speak to your children, and I choose to believe that You have great things for me." Peace flooded my heart as I once again put my trust in God's character and goodness instead of my understanding.

Weakness is not a sickness to be healed.

In response to this experience with my dad's death, as well as other difficult experiences, I decided to create an imaginary box in my mind. I call it the "mystery of God" box. I put things in it that I do not understand, things I cannot figure out, like why I felt I had heard God speak about my dad's death. The more I reflected on all my experiences of God's goodness, the more my heart was filled with trust toward Him. That is why I was able to create that mystery box—because I know God has been good before and that He will be good again.

Putting the experience of my father's death in the "mystery of God" box has allowed me to continue walking in trust and belief in God's goodness. There are things in that box I have peace about without ever knowing why. When I put things in that box, I let them go. I even forget some of them.

Some people say we will be able to bring all our questions to Jesus in heaven. I think that the joy of being with Him, even the very sight of Him, will overwhelm all of our questions and our suffering.

What are the unanswered questions for you? What is the source of your disappointment with God? Maybe there have been tragedies or other traumatic experiences in your life that do not make sense. Maybe you need a "mystery of God" box in your own mind. We all experience pain and suffering in our lives, and perhaps we have let those experiences give us cause to push away from God. If anything, we need to let them push us toward Him, because He shares our pain. He knows our struggle. He is present with us when we endure suffering.

Jesus was no stranger to suffering and weakness. Isaiah said, "He was . . . a man of sorrows, and familiar with suffering" (Isa. 53:3). This was the essence of the incarnation. When God became a man, He made Himself nothing, choosing to identify with human weakness. Our weaknesses became His weakness. Though He was without sin, Jesus experienced the full range of human pain and suffering. He knows what it is to be frail. He has felt every physical and emotional desire we feel. He was tempted in every way that we are tempted (Heb. 4:15). In humility, Jesus did not demand to be treated as someone special, but embraced weakness, taking on the form of a servant (Phil. 2:6–8). This is the path Jesus invites us to walk down as we follow Him. We need to come to terms with our weaknesses and limitations.

The apostle Paul also makes profound claims about his own weakness. In his first letter to the Corinthians, he says, "For I decided that while I was with you I would forget everything except Jesus Christ, the one who was crucified. I came to you in weakness—timid and trembling" (1 Cor. 2:2–3 NLT). I have always put Paul in a heroic William Wallace/Rambo category: an untouchable, bold, strong, raw hero of the faith. Yet in the Scriptures, Paul talks openly about being weak. I want to be like Paul, but I do not want to be weak!

Paul not only admits his weakness; he revels in it, writing, "I take pleasure in my weaknesses" (2 Cor. 12:10 NLT). He embraces the promise Jesus made to him: "My grace is all you need. My power works best in weakness" (2 Cor. 12:9 NLT). Let us imitate Paul. If we have God's call to do something but feel weak, let us run to Jesus, lean on Him, and walk forward, knowing that His power is enough to accomplish everything He wants us to do. Our fears and weaknesses lead us to deeper a knowledge of and trust in Jesus and what He is doing in our lives.

As we embrace our weakness, we get to know God better, and fear loses its power. Weakness is not a sickness to be healed. It is a doorway to the knowledge and power of God. Stepping out, even when we feel weak, enables us to encounter the God of the universe. This is a God who is strong when we are weak, who is good even when we do not understand His ways, who is present in the midst of our fears, who provides for us and protects us, who loves us, and whose love for us is unconditional. This is our God. He calls us forward, though we are weak and afraid, so that we will find Him strong.

Thank You, Jesus, that You are all I need. Help me to embrace my weakness and find your strength. Amen.

chapter eight

The Reality of Jesus

*I*n 2009 I went to Israel. As I was departing from the airport in Tel Aviv, the officials began asking me questions about my stay. At first the questions were normal and routine, but then they asked me to step aside for further questioning. They began asking about my past visits to the Middle East and searched my bags. In one of my suitcases, they found a copy of my book Imprisoned in Iran. This got them really curious. They took my computer, turned it on, and began searching my files. After they had gone through all my possessions, they took me into another room where they asked me to remove my clothes.

Suddenly, I was having flashbacks of my prison experience in Iran. Memories of torture, beatings, and the fear of death came flooding into my mind. As I stood there in my underwear, it became clear to me that I could very well be returning to prison. My body began to shake as I tried to answer their questions. My departure time was getting closer, and I was afraid I would miss my flight. It felt like being back in Iran, when my passport was taken away and I missed the bus that was to take me across the border. Was it all happening again? I began to pray and to cry out to Jesus in my heart.

As I prayed, the guards instructed me to get dressed. I put my clothes on, and they led me outside. I thought I was going to prison. Instead, the officer escorted me directly to my flight gate, where all the other passengers were boarding. He handed me my passport, looked at me with a smile, and said, "Enjoy your flight."

Safely on the plane, I burst into tears of joy. The fear I had felt five minutes earlier, as the Israeli guards searched and questioned me, was real—in some ways, it had felt exactly like being detained in Iran twelve years earlier. But this time I had hope in my heart. Even as memories of trauma resurfaced, powerful memories of Jesus's miraculous intervention had begun filling my heart. I was the same person, but this time I had a deeper hope.

I would love to have complete victory over fear, but making that my primary goal is counterproductive.

Can we really have hope in the face of fear? Yes—absolutely yes! Jesus is our hope!

All of us can find hope in Jesus when we reflect on what He has done in our lives. There are so many experiences in my life that cause hope to arise in my heart when I think back on them. One of these is the story of how Jesus saved me from death in the mountains of Afghanistan.

Eye care is scarce outside the major cities in Afghanistan, and I often led medical teams into remote areas to provide service to the villages. On one trip, I had taken a team of twelve up into the mountains. We hiked for two days to a base camp at about twelve thousand feet. As we passed through a clearing, we walked onto a huge boulder, about the size of a five-story apartment complex. Suddenly, I lost my footing and began sliding down the edge of the boulder. I tried to scramble back up but kept sliding down, picking up speed on the slippery stone. Frantically, I looked for something to grab onto, but there was nothing. I looked down and saw I was quickly approaching a five-hundred-foot drop.

My desire for Jesus needs to be stronger than my desire for victory over fear.

As my feet passed over the edge of the boulder, I knew it was over. I was going to die. In desperation, I thrust my right hand up, grasping for anything. I caught two blades of grass and a thin root peeking out of a crack in the stone. To my surprise, I came to an abrupt halt—the root and grass held! I was dangling five hundred feet above the riverbed, swinging at the edge of the boulder. I clung tightly to the tiny plants for over a minute, my heart pounding. Finally, I realized I was still alive and I had to move. I caught my wits and looked to the left. There was a crack in the boulder. I shoved my left hand in. Then I saw a hold for my right hand. I pulled myself up and found another crack, then another, until finally I reached the top of the boulder, where I collapsed, trembling. I should have died. In that moment, nothing but Jesus could have given me hope. No one but Jesus could have saved my life.

The story gets better. Three years later, at a YWAM conference in Colorado Springs, my friend Silvana came up to me.

"Dan," she said, "was your life in danger three years ago?"

"It's always in danger. I live in Afghanistan," I replied.

"But was your life specifically in danger during the month of August, three years ago?"

I thought back and remembered that August was when I almost fell to my death.

"Yeah. I almost fell off a cliff!"

"Do you remember the exact day?"

"Yes."

"Do you remember the exact hour?"

"Yes. It was right after lunch, more or less."

Silvana's eyes filled with joy.

"Dan! At the moment you were falling off the cliff, God woke me up in Brazil and told me to pray for you, to pray that angels would save your life!"

Silvana pulled out her prayer journal. She opened it to the entry three years ago, at that exact hour, where she had written about praying for angels to save my life! Our eyes filled with tears of joy at God's incredible love and power. This is the source of my hope—I know I am in the hands of a loving God who will always take care of me.

When I encounter fear in my life, I often stop and remember stories like these. The book of Revelation tells us our testimony has power over the enemy: "They overcame [the enemy] because of the blood of the Lamb and because of the word of their testimony" (Rev. 12:11 NASB). As I reflect on my testimony, I begin to focus on who God is. It is then that I see the power of fear broken.

"Jesus Christ is the same yesterday and today and forever" (Heb. 13:8). If God brought victory over fear in the past, I can trust and be confident that He will do it again. All I need to do is keep learning to focus on Jesus instead of on my fear. Of course, I would love to have complete victory over fear, but making that my primary goal is counterproductive. Jesus Himself is the key to that victory. My desire for Jesus needs to be stronger than my desire for victory over fear. Switching my focus from fear to Jesus has been a process and a journey in my life. It has taken time, discipline, and faith. In my experience, however, it does become easier.

The same things that scared me ten years ago, or even twenty years ago, still scare me—but now I am less afraid.

Ultimately, overcoming our fears is entirely dependent upon the hope we have in the love of Jesus. By God's power, despite and even amid our fears, we are all on this journey of becoming more in love with Jesus.

When I pursue Jesus, I soon find myself lost in His beauty and love. Eventually, I realize my fears have started to fade and lose their grip on me. I am less nervous, less worried, and less afraid than I used to be. Am I still vulnerable to fear? Absolutely. The same things that scared me ten years ago, or even twenty years ago, still scare me—but now I am less afraid. Now, as I turn toward God, I see my fears in perspective. I begin to see with the eyes of faith, and I see a God who is bigger, stronger, and more powerful than whatever crisis I am in. I still face fears, but instead of bogging me down, they invite me to run to God. I have learned to trust in God more and more. Because of that, I have hope in the face of fear.

Jesus wants to overwhelm us. He wants to help us overcome our fears with hope in His love and goodness. A few years ago, I was sitting with a friend at the YWAM Kona campus, discussing the goodness of Jesus. "Is there more to know about Jesus and his goodness?" we wondered. "If so, how do we get overwhelmed by it?"

As we talked, we were struck with a funny thought: "What if, right now, twenty elephants started running through the campus?" We laughed and explored the idea further. Assuming no one got hurt, what would happen? Well, we would quit talking and run to see the elephants. All the students would leave their classes, and all the kitchen and administrative staff would stop what they were doing. Basically, the whole campus would shut down because we would all want to see the phenomenon of the running elephants! Even people wrestling with fear at that moment would momentarily forget their fears and rush out to see such a dramatic sight.

Freedom from fear is real! We find it as we gaze on Jesus and become consumed by who He is.

Then we had a realization: Jesus is better than elephants. He is far more awesome, and His glory more dramatic—and He is with us all the time. If a herd of elephants could overtake us with awe and overwhelm our fears, how much more should Jesus?

Every now and then, we have experiences in life that grab every bit of our attention. Yet Jesus is immeasurably better than all of those experiences. We need a bigger vision of God—one that will fascinate and overwhelm our hearts. The more we discover Jesus, the more He will overwhelm every other circumstance in our life—He really is that good.

The power of God doesn't only transform the way we view our present circumstances; it also allows us to look back at past experiences and realize He is greater than whatever hurt or pain those experiences caused.

When I was released from prison, I went to Switzerland to be with my family for two weeks before coming back to the States. During those two weeks, I spent several days hiking in the Alps, enjoying God's creation. There, the realities of my situation in prison started to sink in. I had not thought that Jesus would get me out of prison, but He did. I did not think I would walk freely and enjoy life ever again, but there I was. I did not know if the anxiety I felt in prison would ever end, but it did. Jesus had proven Himself greater than all those uncertainties I had felt! I walked and ran through the Alps, knowing that Jesus was greater than the fears I had encountered in prison. I did not have a care in the world. My cares had all been overwhelmed by a greater reality—Jesus!

This is what it's like to walk with God. When we first discover God is good, we experience joy, peace, and contentment. As time goes on, we see that He is even better than we thought, and we are filled with gratitude. But just when we think we have figured out how good He really is, we discover that He is incredibly more! We think, "Jesus is really good!" But He wants us to discover that He is in fact really, really good. Jesus is always better than we think He is. There is always more of Himself that He wants to show us.

If we have Jesus, we have hope. In Jesus, I have found incredible hope in the face of fear. I have also seen my fears fade as I experience more of His love. Jesus gives us peace in the middle of chaos. He is our strength and security in times of trouble. He knows our weaknesses and meets us in the midst of them.

Whenever we encounter fear of any kind, Jesus invites us into His loving presence. It is in His embrace that we find freedom from fear. Freedom from fear is real! We find it as we gaze on Jesus and become consumed by who He is.

True intimacy with Jesus, as well as the joy that it brings to our hearts, allows us to put our fears in perspective. Our fears may not always disappear the way we would like them to, but running to Jesus always blesses us with something better: a growing relationship with Him. There is nothing in life better than that.

It is all about Jesus—His very presence overwhelms everything else.

Jesus is our ultimate reward. Intimacy with Him is our prize. As followers of Jesus, we believe in a future conclusion to the love story between God and humankind. It will be the consummation of God's desire and ours, and we will call it heaven. More than anything, heaven is about unhindered intimacy between God and us. It is in this promise that we hope.

One of the best accounts of heaven is found in the book of Revelation. In his mind-blowing vision of the eternal city, John points emphatically to Jesus. He says, "I did not see a temple in the city, because the Lord God Almighty and the Lamb are its temple. The city does not need the sun or the moon to shine on it, for the glory of God gives it light, and the Lamb is its lamp" (Rev. 21:22–23). It is all about Jesus—His very presence overwhelms everything else.

"This is eternal life," John writes in his Gospel, "that [we] may know you, the only true God, and Jesus Christ, whom you have sent" (John 17:3). That's it! That is what life is all about. We are meant to concern ourselves completely with Jesus—with knowing Him, loving Him, and enjoying Him, now and forever.

A few years ago, early one morning while I was praying, I was given a vision of God's dream for planet Earth. I began to see cities all over the world: London, Bangkok, Los Angeles,

New Delhi, Zurich, New York, Lhasa, Sydney, Cape Town, and on and on. In each city, I saw thousands upon thousands of young people worshiping God. They looked like normal young people—except that all of them were worshiping in complete freedom. The glory of God was falling on them and on their cities. As they worshiped, God's Spirit filled the air, and the atmosphere was flooded with an indescribable peace and joy—so much so that the worshipers began to glow. Crowds of people began flocking in among the worshipers. They came from their homes, their schools, and their places of work, irresistibly drawn to what was happening.

The fears we face in our lives are
real. But Jesus is more real.

I lay on the floor, trembling at the reality of the heart of God I had just experienced. For me, this was a picture of heaven on earth, and it filled me with incredible hope. Someday we will be overwhelmed by God's love, and people everywhere will be consumed with this one thing. The worship of God will no longer be reserved for church buildings or small gatherings in homes. It will not be private or secret; God's glory will be evident to all. His kingdom will come on earth as it is in heaven, and it will be something far greater than we have ever seen or imagined.

After I saw this vision, I wept for hours. I was overcome with the desire that God has for all of us—to be totally set free to worship Him. When we catch a glimpse of God's glory, nothing else matters. All of our fears and inhibitions fall away, and we begin to experience life as it was meant to be. Nothing compares to that. Once we experience a taste of it, we only want to gaze upon God's beauty forever. The hope of heaven has been, and will be, a beautiful reality that overshadows every fear. Walking in the midst of this increasingly disclosed revelation has changed my life.

The fears we face in our lives are real. But Jesus is more real. He is bigger than we think, and better than we think. That is what life is all about: discovering the never-ending revelation of who Jesus is and allowing that to become greater than every other reality. No matter what fears we have had in the past, no matter what fears we currently face, there is hope. Jesus is our hope. He is in the midst of our fears and calls us to Himself. Fear is a catalyst to run to Jesus. It is an invitation into the most glorious reality in life. That reality is Jesus.

Thank You, Father, for giving me hope in the face of fear. Help me now to take the next step on this journey of discovering Your love. Give me a greater revelation of heaven and the faith to follow You with childlike expectation. Overwhelm me. I want to fall more and more in love with You. Amen.

chapter nine

Walking Out Guidance in the Midst of Fear: A Case Study

*H*ow do you make decisions even when you feel afraid? This case study may help you walk through some of your own fears.

For me, the process of moving to Kabul, Afghanistan, touched on almost every fear I have mentioned in this book. In this case study, we will look at the fears this process brought up in my heart. These are:

- Fear of missing God's will
- Fear of failure
- Fear of disappointment
- Fear of man
- Fear of not having enough money
- Fear of loneliness and of being alone
- Fear that I'm not ready

- Fear of losing control
- Fear of not being safe
- Fear that my actions are out of God's timing

Throughout this case study, I will describe my initial reactions to these fears and discuss three different responses.

The first response I call common sense. When I say common sense, I do not mean that all common sense is bad. God gave us common sense and often calls us to use it. What is bad is when common sense replaces our dependency on Jesus—when we use reason as an excuse to avoid obedience. Proverbs 3:5 makes it very clear: "Trust in the Lord with all your heart and lean not on your own understanding." When "common sense" contradicts what Jesus is saying, it is no longer common sense.

The second response I call personal insecurity. Responding from personal insecurity means replacing reliance upon God with how we feel at the moment. When personal insecurity influences our emotions, trusting God is harder because it requires us to confront fears that have shaped the way we have seen the world for many years.

The final response I call Jesus's encouragement. It is the sense of peace that can accompany us throughout our journey, if we run to Jesus. Some days we sense it more strongly than others. But it is always available, and it is always the best option.

After I describe each fear, I will discuss the decision I ultimately made and/or the outcome.

THE STORY BEGINS when I was twenty-two years old. That year was the first time the prospect of going to Afghanistan came up in my heart. I remember when I started thinking about it. It was completely consistent with guidance God had given me in the past. But over the next few months, I began feeling insecure about my ability to hear God. I had graduated from university with a business degree and with the hope of working in the Middle East. Even though going to Afghanistan seemed to fit into the plans I already had, I still questioned whether or not this was God. All I could do was run back to Him. I remember doing that and hearing absolutely nothing. When I heard no confirmation, I began thinking it was most likely not God's will that I go, even though I still wasn't sure. In other words, I was telling God, "I have to have confirmation. Otherwise I'm not going." I began wrestling with the three responses.

Common Sense
Unless you have numerous confirmations—especially if you are considering going to a dangerous place like Afghanistan—you should assume it isn't God telling you to go.

Personal Insecurity
You've heard God wrong in the past. So, since you're not getting any confirmation, you must be hearing Him wrong again.

Jesus's Encouragement
If you are honest, you already know what to do, despite not having any confirmation. Even though it scares you to walk forward in this, I am your peace. Follow my peace and trust my goodness and faithfulness over your life.

Decision and Outcome
Although I had no clear confirmation, I went forward. In other words, God's peace was greater than having indisputable guidance.

DURING THIS PROCESS, I was often aware of the fear of failure. What if I was making the biggest mistake of my life? What if I was totally missing it? What if, after I got there, it turned out to be a train wreck and I had to come home because nothing went right?

Common Sense
Don't take another step forward until you are absolutely sure you will not fail in any way, shape, or form.

Personal Insecurity
Because of your lack of preparation, business experience, finances, and cultural knowledge, this is doomed to fail.

Jesus's Encouragement
I am more committed to your succeeding than even you are. I never focus on your failures. I am overwhelmed by love for you, and your momentary failures are not what is always on my mind—my destiny for you is.

Decision
I decided to trust in Jesus and in God's calling on my life, so I went ahead and moved forward with the details of the application.

AFTER APPLYING TO the hospital, I was still not 100 percent sure I would be accepted, although they had told me I had a 95 percent chance. They had also told me it would be a few months before I heard back from them. After a few weeks of hearing nothing from them, I began to think, "They are not going to accept me. And since they aren't going to accept me, I should find something else to do." I was afraid of being disappointed and rejected.

Common Sense
You were told to wait a few months for a response. Be patient and wait.

Personal Insecurity
You won't get accepted because you're not qualified. You need to look for something else.

Jesus's Encouragement
I am good. You can trust the peace in your heart.

Decision
I felt a peace to follow my common sense, so I continued to wait for their response.

I HAVE BEEN very grateful for the counsel of others throughout my life, but that does not mean, in every decision, that what others say is right. I remember asking several people whether I should go to Afghanistan or not. A few said, "Follow your heart," but many questioned my guidance. When people questioned whether I was hearing from God, it brought up the fear of man. These were people I loved and respected, and it seemed that their critiques were valid. What if God was bringing them into my life to help me make the right decision?

Common Sense
Follow the advice of those around you; they care for you and obviously know what's best for you.

Personal Insecurity
So many people are saying not to go. Should I go or not?

Jesus's Encouragement
Continue to look to Me and proceed with your original sense of guidance. Listen to other people's concerns and take them into consideration, but follow the peace in your heart—even if it's different from the advice you are receiving.

Decision
I decided to pursue Jesus's leading toward Afghanistan.

ANOTHER FEAR THAT came my way regularly was the fear of not having enough money. The job I was considering was a volunteer position, and I was told I needed $1,000 a month at minimum to live in Kabul. I did not yet have the money, so what was I going to do?

Common Sense
Wait till you have the money before you go.

Personal Insecurity
You're not getting the money you need. This must be a sign that God doesn't want you to go.

Jesus's Encouragement
"Seek first my kingdom and my righteousness, and all these things will be given to you as well."

Decision and Outcome
I decided to go ahead, even without certainty of financial provision. During my entire time in Afghanistan, God always provided for me. I never lacked anything.

DURING THE SEVEN months between graduation and leaving for Kabul, I often dealt with the fear of being alone and what it would look like when I got to Afghanistan. I was afraid of being abandoned and not having any friends. The loneliness was real, and often it was overwhelming.

Common Sense
If you are going to move into an environment that is so far from home and presents so many challenges, it would be best for you to get married before you go. At least bring a close friend with you. Don't go unless you have companionship.

Personal Insecurity
You won't be able to handle the loneliness, and you will be totally depressed. Don't go!

Jesus's Encouragement
Ask me for fresh revelation of how much I love you. I long to show you how much I love you and to take care of all your relational needs.

Outcome
During my time in Afghanistan, I made some of the closest friendships of my life. Although I never got married, and although I struggled at times with loneliness, my friendship with Jesus was very real. Jesus satisfied my heart at the deepest level, and that is what I truly wanted.

IF YOU WOULD have asked me what the next seven months should look like as I prepared to go to Afghanistan, I would have said, "I want to grow in many personal areas of my life. I want to be more confident in hearing God's voice and in my Bible knowledge, to see more fruit of the Spirit in my life, and to have complete victory over struggles with personal sin." Basically, I wanted to look and feel more like a man of God before I got on that airplane. I needed to overcome my fear of not being ready.

Common Sense

Don't go until you feel ready to go. Don't go unless you feel godly, you've conquered your insecurities and sin struggles, and the fruit of the Spirit is beaming through your life.

Personal Insecurity

You're not ready to go! You still struggle with sin. There are still so many areas of your character that are not in line with Jesus's character. You need more time to become more godly before you can go.

Jesus's Encouragement

Whether you feel ready or not, you are ready because I have called you. "For it is by grace you have been saved, through faith—and this not from yourselves, it is the gift of God—not by works, so that no one can boast" (Eph. 2:8–9). "He who began a good work in you will carry it on to completion until the day of Christ Jesus" (Phil. 1:6). I know you are ready to go, because I told you to go. You need to trust that I, in you, am enough. What makes you ready is my call on your life, not your confidence or lack of confidence in yourself.

Outcome

Would I ever have been "ready" to go to Afghanistan? I am so glad I walked forward, putting my confidence in God's grace and His work in my life. In fact, by obeying God in this calling, I naturally grew in the areas I needed to grow in.

AS I WALKED out those seven months before going, I was accosted by fears, at any given moment, that caused me to feel like I was losing control. The fear of not being in control often paralyzed me. In May I began preparing to go to Afghanistan, and I quickly made a mental checklist of how things should go by January: I had to have all my finances raised by September, positive opinions from 90 to 95 percent of other people, be married by January, and do everything else I could to "feel ready." I had defined these as requirements before the Lord, even though He had not made them so. In reality, when January came, I had only 20 percent of the voluntary donation commitments I would need, over 50 percent of the people I knew were still fearful for my safety and discouraging me from going, and I was not only unmarried but also going to Afghanistan alone. Moreover, I felt completely emotionally unprepared to go. Everything felt out of control.

Common Sense
Unless you're in control and can foresee the outcome of your actions, don't move forward.

Personal Insecurity
There's no way you'll be able to handle life unless all these requirements are met.

Jesus's Encouragement
Commit to trust me despite how you feel and despite the circumstances. I am a good shepherd, and I will always lead you toward what is best.

Outcome
The freedom God gave me as I relinquished control was so life-giving. Trusting Him at every level brought great joy to my heart.

WAR WAS RAGING in Afghanistan, and conditions were worse than they are today. I began fearing for my personal safety. I often thought, "What if I die while I am there?"

Common Sense
Don't go unless your safety is guaranteed.

Personal Insecurity
It's dangerous! I'd be stupid to go. Come on, I don't need to ask God—it's obvious!

Jesus's Encouragement
I will take care of you. "If you say 'the Lord is my refuge,' and you make the Most High your dwelling, no harm will overtake you, no disaster will come near your tent" (Ps. 91:9–10).

Outcome
God always protected me, even in some very dangerous situations.

AS MY DEPARTURE date drew closer, I had moments when the "timing question" popped into my head. Is this the right time to go? I was afraid God would not take care of me if I was not operating under His perfect timing.

Common Sense
Of course it's not the right timing. It's not safe, you don't have the money, and you're struggling with loneliness!

Personal Insecurity
Maybe I should question my sense of God's guidance because it doesn't feel as good as I want it to feel.

Jesus's Encouragement
My timing is perfect. Follow the peace I put in your heart.

Outcome
From the day I went to Afghanistan until the day I left, I knew in my heart of hearts that it was the right time to be there. I never regretted one moment of being there. Although I didn't feel it every day, God's joy, peace, and fulfillment caused me to have confidence that it was the right time to be there.

IF I AM completely honest, many of the fears I faced in those seven months caused me to doubt God's goodness. I was often tempted to think, "Where God is leading me probably can't be the best place for me." Now, of course, it is faithless to say that, but it is what we are tempted to think sometimes. God knows what is best for us, in all things. He is a good Father, and He wants to prove His goodness to us. Jesus declares the Father's extravagant goodness when He says, "If you, then, though you are evil, know how to give good gifts to your children, how much more will your Father in heaven give good gifts to those who ask him!" (Matt. 7:11).

Every step of obedience toward what God told me to do diminished my awareness of fear and increased my awe of God. As I saw my fears lose their influence, I grew in confidence that God was good, that He was with me, and that He would take care of me. It is really that simple. God loves us, and we get to love Him back! We do that by living in obedience. When fear prevents us from following His direction, or the effort to overcome it becomes a distraction, we miss living with simple obedience. There is no fear that should keep us from obeying God. He wants us to follow Him even with our fears. In doing so, we will discover more and more of how wonderful He is.